LOVE CONQUERS ALL

They look him over as if he were a fresh air child being
given a day's outing.

LOVE
CONQUERS ALL

BY
ROBERT C. BENCHLEY

ILLUSTRATED BY
GLUYAS WILLIAMS

A COMMON READER EDITION
THE AKADINE PRESS

Love Conquers All

ACKNOWLEDGMENT

The author thanks the editors of the following publications for their permission to print the articles in this book: *Life, The New York World, The New York Tribune, The Detroit Athletic Club News, and The Consolidated Press Association.*

CONTENTS

v

CONTENTS

vi

CONTENTS

ILLUSTRATIONS

LOVE CONQUERS ALL

I

THE BENCHLEY–WHITTIER CORRE-
SPONDENCE

OLD scandals concerning the private life of Lord Byron have been revived with the recent publication of a collection of his letters. One of the big questions seems to be: *Did Byron send Mary Shelley's letter to Mrs. R. B. Hoppner?* Everyone seems greatly excited about it.

Lest future generations be thrown into turmoil over my correspondence after I am gone, I want right now to clear up the mystery which has puzzled literary circles for over thirty years. I need hardly add that I refer to what is known as the " Benchley-Whittier Correspondence."

The big question over which both my biographers and Whittier's might possibly come to blows is this, as I understand it: *Did John Greenleaf Whittier ever receive the letters I wrote to him in the late Fall of* 1890? *If he did not, who did? And under what circumstances were they written?*

I was a very young man at the time, and Mr. Whittier was, naturally, very old. There had been a meeting of the Save-Our-Song-Birds Club in old Dane Hall (now demolished) in Cambridge, Massachusetts. Members had left their coats and hats in the check-room at the foot of the stairs (now demolished).

In passing out after a rather spirited meeting, during the course of which Mr. Whittier and Dr. Van Blarcom had opposed each other rather violently over the question of Baltimore orioles, the aged poet naturally was the first to be helped into his coat. In the general mix-up (there was considerable good-natured fooling among the members as they left, relieved as they were from the strain of the meeting) Whittier was given my hat by mistake. When I came to go, there was nothing left for me but a rather seedy gray derby with a black band, containing the initials " J. G. W." As the poet was visiting in Cambridge at the time I took opportunity next day to write the following letter to him:

Cambridge, Mass.
November 7, 1890.

Dear Mr. Whittier:

I am afraid that in the confusion following the Save-Our-Song-Birds meeting last night, you were given my hat by mistake. I have yours and will gladly exchange it if you will let me know when I may call on you.

May I not add that I am a great admirer of your verse? Have you ever tried any musical comedy lyrics? I think that I could get you in on the ground floor in the show game, as I know a young man who has written several songs which E. E. Rice has said he would like to use in his next comic opera — provided he can get words to go with them.

But we can discuss all this at our meeting, which I hope will be soon, as your hat looks like hell on me.

Yours respectfully,

ROBERT C. BENCHLEY.

I am quite sure that this letter was mailed, as I find an entry in my diary of that date which reads:

" Mailed a letter to J. G. Whittier. Cloudy and cooler."

Furthermore, in a death-bed confession, some ten years later, one Mary F. Rourke, a servant employed in the house of Dr. Agassiz, with whom Whittier was bunking at the time, admitted that she herself had taken a letter, bearing my name in

the corner of the envelope, to the poet at his breakfast on the following morning.

But whatever became of it after it fell into his
hands, I received no reply. I waited five days, during which time I stayed in the house rather than go
out wearing the Whittier gray derby. On the sixth
day I wrote him again, as follows:

Cambridge, Mass.
Nov. 14, 1890.

Dear Mr. Whittier:

    How about that hat of mine?

Yours respectfully,
ROBERT C. BENCHLEY.

I received no answer to this letter either. Con-
cluding that the good gray poet was either too busy
or too gosh-darned mean to bother with the thing,
I myself adopted an attitude of supercilious uncon-
cern and closed the correspondence with the following terse message:

Cambridge, Mass.
December 4, 1890.

Dear Mr. Whittier:

    It is my earnest wish that the hat of mine which
you are keeping will slip down over your eyes some
day, interfering with your vision to such an

extent that you will walk off the sidewalk into the gutter and receive painful, albeit superficial, injuries.

Your young friend,

ROBERT C. BENCHLEY.

Here the matter ended so far as I was concerned, and I trust that biographers in the future will not let any confusion of motives or misunderstanding of dates enter into a clear and unbiased statement of the whole affair. We must not have another Shelley-Byron scandal.

II

FAMILY LIFE IN AMERICA

Part 1

The naturalistic literature of this country has reached such a state that no family of characters is considered true to life which does not include at least two hypochondriacs, one sadist, and one old man who spills food down the front of his vest. If this school progresses, the following is what we may expect in our national literature in a year or so.

THE living-room in the Twillys' house was so damp that thick, soppy moss grew all over the walls. It dripped on the picture of Grandfather Twilly that hung over the melodeon, making streaks down the dirty glass like sweat on the old man's face. It was a mean face. Grandfather Twilly had been a mean man and had little spots of soup on the lapel of his coat. All his children were mean and had soup spots on their clothes.

Grandma Twilly sat in the rocker over by the window, and as she rocked the chair snapped. It sounded like Grandma Twilly's knees snapping as they did whenever she stooped over to pull the wings off a fly. She was a mean old thing. Her knuckles were grimy and she chewed crumbs that

[8]

she found in the bottom of her reticule. You would
have hated her. She hated herself. But most of
all she hated Grandfather Twilly.

" I certainly hope you're frying good," she muttered as she looked up at his picture.

" Hasn't the undertaker come yet, Ma? " asked
young Mrs. Wilbur Twilly petulantly. She was
boiling water on the oil-heater and every now and
again would spill a little of the steaming liquid on
the baby who was playing on the floor. She hated
the baby because it looked like her father. The
hot water raised little white blisters on the baby's
red neck and Mabel Twilly felt short, sharp twinges
of pleasure at the sight. It was the only pleasure
she had had for four months.

" Why don't you kill yourself, Ma? " she continued. " You're only in the way here and you
know it. It's just because you're a mean old woman
and want to make trouble for us that you hang on."

Grandma Twilly shot a dirty look at her daugh-
ter-in-law. She had always hated her. Stringy
hair, Mabel had. Dank, stringy hair. Grandma
Twilly thought how it would look hanging at an
Indian's belt. But all that she did was to place her
tongue against her two front teeth and make a noise
like the bath-room faucet.

[9]

LOVE CONQUERS ALL

Wilbur Twilly was reading the paper by the oil lamp. Wilbur had watery blue eyes and cigar ashes all over his knees. The third and fourth buttons of his vest were undone. It was too hideous.

He was conscious of his family seated in chairs about him. His mother, chewing crumbs. His wife Mabel, with her stringy hair, reading. His sister Bernice, with projecting front teeth, who sat thinking of the man who came every day to take away the waste paper. Bernice was wondering how long it would be before her family would discover that she had been married to this man for three years.

How Wilbur hated them all. It didn't seem as if he could stand it any longer. He wanted to scream and stick pins into every one of them and then rush out and see the girl who worked in his office snapping rubber-bands all day. He hated her too, but she wore side-combs.

PART 2

The street was covered with slimy mud. It oozed out from under Bernice's rubbers in unpleasant bubbles until it seemed to her as if she must kill herself. Hot air coming out from a steam laundry. Hot, stifling air. Bernice didn't work in the laundry but she wished that she did so that the hot air would kill her. She wanted to be stifled. She needed torture to be happy. She also needed a good swift clout on the side of the face.

A drunken man lurched out from a door-way and flung his arms about her. It was only her husband. She loved her husband. She loved him so much that, as she pushed him away and into the gutter, she stuck her little finger into his eye. She also untied his neck-tie. It was a bow neck-tie, with white, dirty spots on it and it was wet with gin. It didn't seem as if Bernice could stand it any longer. All the repressions of nineteen sordid years behind protruding teeth surged through her untidy soul. She wanted love. But it was not her husband that she loved so fiercely. It was old Grandfather Twilly. And he was too dead.

PART 3

In the dining-room of the Twillys' house every-thing was very quiet. Even the vinegar-cruet which was covered with fly-specks. Grandma Twilly lay with her head in the baked potatoes, poisoned by Mabel, who, in her turn had been poisoned by her husband and sprawled in an odd posture over the china-closet. Wilbur and his sister Bernice had

just finished choking each other to death and between them completely covered the carpet in that
corner of the room where the worn spot showed the
bare boards beneath, like ribs on a chicken carcass.

Only the baby survived. She had a mean face
and had great spillings of Imperial Granum down
her bib. As she looked about her at her family, a
great hate surged through her tiny body and her
eyes snapped viciously. She wanted to get down
from her high-chair and show them all how much
she hated them.

Bernice's husband, the man who came after the
waste paper, staggered into the room. The tips
were off both his shoe-lacings. The baby experi-
enced a voluptuous sense of futility at the sight of
the tipless-lacings and leered suggestively at her
uncle-in-law.

" We must get the roof fixed," said the man, very
quietly. " It lets the sun in."

III

THIS CHILD KNOWS THE ANSWER —
DO YOU?

WE are occasionally confronted in the advertisements by the picture of an offensively bright-looking little boy, fairly popping with information, who, it is claimed in the text, knows all the inside dope on why fog forms in beads on a woolen coat, how long it would take to crawl to the moon on your hands and knees, and what makes oysters so quiet.

The taunting catch-line of the advertisement is: " This Child Knows the Answer — Do You? " and the idea is to shame you into buying a set of books containing answers to all the questions in the world except the question " Where is the money coming from to buy the books? "

Any little boy knowing all these facts would unquestionably be an asset in a business which specialized in fog-beads or lunar transportation novelties, but he would be awful to have about the house.

" Spencer," you might say to him, " where are Daddy's slippers? " To which he would undoubtedly answer: "I don't know, Dad," (disagreeable little boys like that always call their fathers "Dad" and stand with their feet wide apart and their hands in their pockets like girls playing boys' rôles on the stage) "but I *do* know this, that all the Nordic peoples are predisposed to astigmatism because of the glare of the sun on the snow, and that, furthermore, if you were to place a common ordinary marble in a glass of luke-warm cider there would be a precipitation which, on pouring off the cider, would be found to be what we know as parsley, just plain parsley which Cook uses every night in preparing our dinner."

With little ones like this around the house, a new version of "The Children's Hour" will have to be arranged, and it might as well be done now and got over with.

The Well-Informed Children's Hour

Between the dark and the day-light,
When the night is beginning to lower,
Comes a pause in the day's occupation
Which is known as the children's hour.
'Tis then appears tiny Irving
With the patter of little feet,
To tell us that worms become dizzy
At a slight application of heat.

THIS CHILD KNOWS THE ANSWER

And Norma, the baby savant,
Comes toddling up with the news
That a valvular catch in the larynx
Is the reason why Kitty mews.
" Oh Grandpa," cries lovable Lester,
" Jack Frost has surprised us again,
By condensing in crystal formation
The vapor which clings to the pane! "
Then Roger and Lispinard Junior
Race pantingly down through the hall
To be first with the hot information
That bees shed their coats in the Fall.
No longer they clamor for stories
As they cluster in fun 'round my knee
But each little darling is bursting
With a story that he must tell me,
Giving reasons why daisies are sexless
And what makes the turtle so dour;
So it goes through the horrible gloaming
Of the Well-Informed Children's Hour.

IV

RULES AND SUGGESTIONS FOR WATCH-
ING AUCTION BRIDGE

WITH all the expert advice that is being offered in print these days about how to play games, it seems odd that no one has formulated a set of rules for the spectators. The spectators are much more numerous than the players, and seem to need more regulation. As a spectator of twenty years standing, versed in watching all sports except six-day bicycle races, I offer the fruit of my experience in the form of suggestions and reminiscences which may tend to clarify the situation, or, in case there is no situation which needs clarifying, to make one.

In the event of a favorable reaction on the part of the public, I shall form an association, to be known as the National Amateur Audience Association (or the N. A. A. A., if you are given to slang) of which I shall be Treasurer. That's all I ask, the Treasurership.

This being an off-season of the year for outdoor sports (except walking, which is getting to have neither participants nor spectators) it seems best to start with a few remarks on the strenuous occupation of watching a bridge game. Bridge-watchers are not so numerous as football watchers, for instance, but they are much more in need of coordination and it will be the aim of this article to formulate a standardized set of rules for watching bridge which may be taken as a criterion for the whole country.

NUMBER WHO MAY WATCH

There should not be more than one watcher for each table. When there are two, or more, confusion is apt to result and no one of the watchers can devote his attention to the game as it should be devoted. Two watchers are also likely to bump into each other as they make their way around the table looking over the players' shoulders. If there are more watchers than there are tables, two can share one table between them, one being dummy while the other watches. In this event the first one should watch until the hand has been dealt and six tricks taken, being relieved by the second one for the remaining tricks and the marking down of the score.

LOVE CONQUERS ALL

PRELIMINARIES

In order to avoid any charge of signalling, it will be well for the following conversational formula to be used before the game begins:

The ring-leader of the game says to the fifth person: "Won't you join the game and make a fourth? I have some work which I really ought to be doing."

The fifth person replies: "Oh, no, thank you! I play a wretched game. I'd much rather sit here and read, if you don't mind."

To which the ring-leader replies: "Pray do."

After the first hand has been dealt, the fifth person, whom we shall now call the "watcher," puts down the book and leans forward in his (or her) chair, craning the neck to see what is in the hand nearest him. The strain becoming too great, he arises and approaches the table, saying: "Do you mind if I watch a bit?"

No answer need be given to this, unless someone at the table has nerve enough to tell the truth.

PROCEDURE

The game is now on. The watcher walks around the table, giving each hand a careful scrutiny, groaning slightly at the sight of a poor one and making

The watcher walks around the table, giving each hand a
careful scrutiny.

noises of joyful anticipation at the good ones. Stopping behind an especially unpromising array of cards, it is well to say: " Well, unlucky at cards, lucky in love, you know." This gives the partner an opportunity to judge his chances on the bid he is about to make, and is perfectly fair to the other side, too, for they are not left entirely in the dark. Thus everyone benefits by the remark.

When the bidding begins, the watcher has considerable opportunity for effective work. Having seen how the cards lie, he is able to stand back and listen with a knowing expression, laughing at unjustified bids and urging on those who should, in his estimation, plunge. At the conclusion of the bidding he should say: " Well, we're off! "

As the hand progresses and the players become intent on the game, the watcher may be the cause of no little innocent diversion. He may ask one of the players for a match, or, standing behind the one who is playing the hand, he may say:

" I'll give you three guesses as to whom I ran into on the street yesterday. Someone you all know. Used to go to school with you, Harry . . . Light hair and blue eyes . . . Medium build . . . Well, sir, it was Lew Milliken. Yessir, Lew Milliken. Hadn't seen him for fifteen years. Asked after you,

Harry . . . and George too. And what do you think he told me about Chick? ”

Answers may or may not be returned to these remarks, according to the good nature of the players, but in any event, they serve their purpose of distraction.

Particular care should be taken that no one of the players is allowed to make a mistake. The watcher, having his mind free, is naturally in a better position to keep track of matters of sequence and revoking. Thus, he may say:

“ The lead was over here, George,” or

“ I think that you refused spades a few hands ago, Lillian.”

Of course, there are some watchers who have an inherited delicacy about offering advice or talking to the players. Some people are that way. They are interested in the game, and love to watch but they feel that they ought not to interfere. I had a cousin who just wouldn't talk while a hand was being played, and so, as she had to do something, she hummed. She didn't hum very well, and her program was limited to the first two lines of “ How Firm a Foundation,” but she carried it off very well and often got the players to humming it along with her. She could also drum rather well with her fingers on the back of the chair of one of the players while looking over his shoulder. "How Firm a Foundation" didn't lend itself very well to drumming; so she had a little patrol that she worked up all by herself, beginning soft, like a drum corps in the distance, and getting louder and louder, finally dying away again so that you could barely hear it. It was wonderful how she could do it — and still go on living.

Those who feel this way about talking while others are playing bridge have a great advantage over my cousin and her class if they can play the piano. They play ever so softly, in order not to disturb, but somehow or other you just know that they are there, and that the next to last note in the coda is going to be very sour.

But, of course, the piano work does not technically come under the head of watching, although when there are two watchers to a table, one may go over to the piano while she is dummy.

But your real watcher will allow nothing to interfere with his conscientious following of the game, and it is for real watchers only that these suggestions have been formulated. The minute you get out of the class of those who have the best interests of the game at heart, you become involved in dilettantism and amateurishness, and the whole sport of bridge-watching falls into disrepute.

LOVE CONQUERS ALL

The only trouble with the game as it now stands is the risk of personal injury. This can be eliminated by the watcher insisting on each player being frisked for weapons before the game begins and cultivating a good serviceable defense against ordinary forms of fistic attack.

V

A CHRISTMAS SPECTACLE

For Use in Christmas Eve Entertainments in the Vestry

AT the opening of the entertainment the Superintendent will step into the footlights, recover
his balance apologetically, and say:

" Boys and girls of the Intermediate Department,
parents and friends: I suppose you all know why
we are here tonight. (At this point the audience
will titter apprehensively). Mrs. Drury and her
class of little girls have been working very hard
to make this entertainment a success, and I am sure
that everyone here to-night is going to have what
I overheard one of my boys the other day calling
' some good time.' (Indulgent laughter from the
little boys). And may I add before the curtain goes
up that immediately after the entertainment we
want you all to file out into the Christian Endeavor room, where there will be a Christmas tree,
' with all the fixin's,' as the boys say." (Shrill
whistling from the little boys and immoderate applause from everyone).

LOVE CONQUERS ALL

There will then be a wait of twenty-five minutes, while sounds of hammering and dropping may be heard from behind the curtains. The Boys' Club orchestra will render the " Poet and Peasant Over-ture " four times in succession, each time differently.

At last one side of the curtains will be drawn back; the other will catch on something and have to be released by hand; someone will whisper loudly, " Put out the lights," following which the entire house will be plunged into darkness. Amid catcalls from the little boys, the footlights will at last go on, disclosing:

The windows in the rear of the vestry rather ineffectively concealed by a group of small fir trees on standards, one of which has already fallen over, leaving exposed a corner of the map of Palestine and the list of gold-star classes for November. In the center of the stage is a larger tree, undecorated, while at the extreme left, invisible to everyone in the audience except those sitting at the extreme right, is an imitation fireplace, leaning against the wall.

Twenty-five seconds too early little Flora Roches-ter will prance out from the wings, uttering the first shrill notes of a song, and will have to be grabbed by eager hands and pulled back. Twenty-four seconds later the piano will begin " The Return of the Reindeer " with a powerful accent on the first note of each bar, and Flora Rochester, Lillian McNulty, Gertrude Hamingham and Martha Wrist will swirl on, dressed in white, and advance heavily into the footlights, which will go out.

There will then be an interlude while Mr. Neff, the sexton, adjusts the connection, during which the four little girls stand undecided whether to brave it out or cry. As a compromise they giggle and are herded back into the wings by Mrs. Drury, amid applause. When the lights go on again, the applause becomes deafening, and as Mr. Neff walks triumphantly away, the little boys in the audience will whistle: "There she goes, there she goes, all dressed up in her Sunday clothes! "

" The Return of the Reindeer " will be started again and the show-girls will reappear, this time more gingerly and somewhat dispirited. They will, however, sing the following, to the music of the " Ballet Pizzicato " from " Sylvia ":

> "We greet you, we greet you,
> On this Christmas Eve so fine.
> We greet you, we greet you,
> And wish you a good time."

They will then turn toward the tree and Flora Rochester will advance, hanging a silver star on one

of the branches, meanwhile reciting a verse, the
only distinguishable words of which are: *" I am
Faith so strong and pure — "*

At the conclusion of her recitation, the star will
fall off.

Lillian McNulty will then step forward and hang
her star on a branch, reading her lines in clear
tones:

" And I am Hope, a virtue great,
My gift to Christmas now I make,
That children and grown-ups may hope today
That tomorrow will be a merry Christmas Day."

The hanging of the third star will be consum-
mated by Gertrude Hamingham, who will get as far
as *" Sweet Charity I bring to place upon the*
tree — " at which point the strain will become too
great and she will forget the remainder. After
several frantic glances toward the wings, from
which Mrs. Drury is sending out whispered mes-
sages to the effect that the next line begins, *" My*
message bright — " Gertrude will disappear, crying
softly.

After the morale of the cast has been in some
measure restored by the pianist, who, with great
presence of mind, plays a few bars of " Will There
Be Any Stars In My Crown? " to cover up Ger-

" 'Round and 'round the tree I go."

trude's exit, Martha Wrist will unleash a rope of silver tinsel from the foot of the tree, and, stringing it over the boughs as she skips around in a circle, will say, with great assurance:

> *" ' Round and 'round the tree I go,*
> *Through the holly and the snow*
> *Bringing love and Christmas cheer*
> *Through the happy year to come."*

At this point there will be a great commotion and jangling of sleigh-bells off-stage, and Mr. Creamer, rather poorly disguised as Santa Claus, will emerge from the opening in the imitation fireplace. A great popular demonstration for Mr. Creamer will follow. He will then advance to the footlights, and, rubbing his pillow and ducking his knees to denote joviality, will say thickly through his false beard:

"Well, well, well, what have we here? A lot of bad little boys and girls who aren't going to get any Christmas presents this year? (Nervous laughter from the little boys and girls). Let me see, let me see! I have a note here from Dr. Whidden. Let's see what it says. (Reads from a paper on which there is obviously nothing written). ' If you and the young people of the Intermediate Department will come into the Christian Endeavor

room, I think we may have a little surprise for you.
. . .' Well, well, well! What do you suppose it
can be? (Cries of " I know, I know! " from so-
phisticated ones in the audience). Maybe it is a
bottle of castor-oil! (Raucous jeers from the little
boys and elaborately simulated disgust on the part
of the little girls.) Well, anyway, suppose we go
out and see? Now if Miss Liftnagle will oblige us
with a little march on the piano, we will all form
in single file — "

At this point there will ensue a stampede toward
the Christian Endeavor room, in which chairs will
be broken, decorations demolished, and the protest-
ing Mr. Creamer badly hurt.

This will bring to a close the first part of the
entertainment.

VI

HOW TO WATCH A CHESS–MATCH

SECOND in the list of games which it is necessary for every sportsman to know how to watch
comes chess. If you don't know how to watch
chess, the chances are that you will never have any
connection with the game whatsoever. You would
not, by any chance, be playing it yourself.

I know some very nice people that play chess,
mind you, and I wouldn't have thought that I was
in any way spoofing at the game. I would sooner
spoof at the people who engineered the Panama
Canal or who are drawing up plans for the vehicular
tunnel under the Hudson River. I am no man to
make light of chess and its adherents, although they
might very well make light of me. In fact, they
have.

But what I say is, that taking society by and
large, man and boy, the chances are that chess
would be the Farmer-Labor Party among the contestants for sporting honors.

Now, since it is settled that you probably will
not want to play chess, unless you should be laid

up with a bad knee-pan or something, it follows that, if you want to know anything about the sport at all, you will have to watch it from the side-lines. That is what this series of lessons aims to teach you to do, (of course, if you are going to be nasty and say that you don't want even to watch it, why all this time has been wasted on my part as well as on yours).

How To Find A Game To Watch

The first problem confronting the chess spectator is to find some people who are playing. The bigger the city, the harder it is to find anyone indulging in chess. In a small town you can usually go straight to Wilbur Tatnuck's General Store, and be fairly sure of finding a quiet game in progress over behind the stove and the crate of pilot-biscuit, but as you draw away from the mitten district you find the sporting instinct of the population cropping out in other lines and chess becoming more and more restricted to the sheltered corners of Y. M. C. A. club-rooms and exclusive social organizations.

However, we shall have to suppose, in order to get any article written at all, that you have found two people playing chess somewhere. They probably will neither see nor hear you as you come up

on them so you can stand directly behind the one
who is defending the south goal without fear of
detection.

The Details Of The Game

At first you may think that they are both dead,
but a mirror held to the lips of the nearest contest-
ant will probably show moisture (unless, of course,
they really should be dead, which would be a horrible ending for a little lark like this. I once
heard of a murderer who propped his two victims
up against a chess board in sporting attitudes and
was able to get as far as Seattle before his crime
was discovered).

Soon you will observe a slight twitching of an
eye-lid or a moistening of the lips and then, like
a greatly retarded moving-picture of a person passing the salt, one of the players will lift a chess-man
from one spot on the board and place it on another
spot.

It would be best not to stand too close to the
board at this time as you are are likely to be tram-
pled on in the excitement. For this action that
you have just witnessed corresponds to a run around
right end in a football game or a two-bagger in
baseball, and is likely to cause considerable enthu-

siasm on the one hand and deep depression on the other. They may even forget themselves to the point of shifting their feet or changing the hands on which they are resting their foreheads. Almost anything is liable to happen.

When the commotion has died down a little, it will be safe for you to walk around and stand behind the other player and wait there for the next move. While waiting it would be best to stand with the weight of your body evenly distributed between your two feet, for you will probably be standing there a long time and if you bear down on one foot all of the time, that foot is bound to get tired. A comfortable stance for watching chess is with the feet slightly apart (perhaps a foot or a foot and a half), with a slight bend at the knees to rest the legs and the weight of the body thrown forward on the balls of the feet. A rhythmic rising on the toes, holding the hands behind the back, the head well up and the chest out, introduces a note of variety into the position which will be welcome along about dusk.

Not knowing anything about the game, you will perhaps find it difficult at first to keep your attention on the board. This can be accomplished by means of several little optical tricks. For instance, if you look at the black and white squares on the board very hard and for a very long time, they will appear to jump about and change places. The black squares will rise from the board about a quarter of an inch and slightly overlap the white ones. Then, if you change focus suddenly, the white squares will do the same thing to the black ones. And finally, after doing this until someone asks you what you are looking cross-eyed for, if you will shut your eyes tight you will see an exact reproduction of the chess-board, done in pink and green, in your mind's eye. By this time, the players will be almost ready for another move.

This will make two moves that you have watched. It is now time to get a little fancy work into your game. About an hour will have already gone by and you should be so thoroughly grounded in the fundamentals of chess watching that you can proceed to the next step.

Have some one of your friends bring you a chair, a table and an old pyrography outfit, together with some book-ends on which to burn a design.

Seat yourself at the table in the chair and (if I remember the process correctly) squeeze the bulb attached to the needle until the latter becomes red hot. Then, grasping the book-ends in the left hand, carefully trace around the pencilled design with the point of the needle. It probably will be a picture of the Lion of Lucerne, and you will let the needle slip on the way round the face, giving it the appearance of having shaved in a Pullman that morning. But that really won't make any difference, for the whole thing is not so much to do a nice pair of book-ends as to help you along in watching the chess-match.

If you have any scruples against burning wood, you may knit something, or paste stamps in an album.

And before you know it, the game will be over and you can put on your things and go home.

VII

WATCHING BASEBALL

D. A. C. NEWS

EIGHTEEN men play a game of baseball and eighteen thousand watch them, and yet those who play are the only ones who have any official direction in the matter of rules and regulations. The eighteen thousand are allowed to run wild. They don't have even a Spalding's Guide containing group photographs of model organizations of fans in Fall River, Mass., or the Junior Rooters of Lyons, Nebraska. Whatever course of behavior a fan follows at a game he makes up for himself. This is, of course, ridiculous.

The first set of official rulings for spectators at baseball games has been formulated and is herewith reproduced. It is to be hoped that in the general clean-up which the game is undergoing, the grandstand and bleachers will not resent a little dictation from the authorities.

In the first place, there is the question of shouting encouragement, or otherwise, at the players.   There must be no more random screaming. It is of course understood that the players are entirely dependent on the advice offered them from the stands for their actions in the game, and how is a batter to know what to do if, for instance, he hears a little man in the bleachers shouting, "Wait for 'em, Wally! Wait for 'em," and another little man in the south stand shouting "Take a crack at the first one, Wally! "? What would you do? What would Lincoln have done?

The official advisers in the stands must work together. They must remember that as the batter advances toward the plate he is listening for them to give him his instructions, and if he hears conflicting advice there is no telling what he may do. He may even have to decide for himself.

Therefore, before each player goes to bat, there should be a conference among the fans who have ideas on what his course of action should be, and as soon as a majority have come to a decision, the advice should be shouted to the player in unison under the direction of a cheer-leader. If there are any dissenting opinions, they may be expressed in a minority report.

In the matter of hostile remarks addressed at an unpopular player on the visiting team it would probably be better to leave the wording entirely to the individual fans. Each man has his own talents in this sort of thing and should be allowed to develop them along natural lines. In such crises as these in which it becomes necessary to rattle the opposing pitcher or prevent the visiting catcher from getting a difficult foul, all considerations of good sportsmanship should be discarded. As a matter of fact, it is doubtful if good sportsmanship should ever be allowed to interfere with the fan's participation in a contest. The game must be kept free from all softening influences.

One of the chief duties of the fan is to engage in arguments with the man behind him. This department of the game has been allowed to run down fearfully. A great many men go to a ball game today and never speak a word to anyone other than the members of their own party or an occasional word of cheer to a player. This is nothing short of craven.

An ardent supporter of the home-team should go to a game prepared to take offense, no matter what happens. He should be equipped with a stock of ready sallies which can be used regardless of what the argument is about or what has gone before in the exchange of words. Among the more popular nuggets of repartee, effective on all occasions, are the following:

" Oh, is that so? "

" Eah? "

" How do you get that way? "

" Oh, is that so? "

" So are you."

" Aw, go have your hair bobbed."

" Oh, is that so? "

" Well, what are you going to do about it? "

" Who says so? "

" Eah?   Well, I'll Cincinnati you."

" Oh, is that so? "

Any one of these, if hurled with sufficient venom, is good for ten points. And it should always be borne in mind that there is no danger of physical harm resulting from even the most ferocious-sounding argument. Statistics gathered by the War Department show that the percentage of actual blows struck in grandstand arguments is one in every 43,000,000.

For those fans who are occasionally obliged to take inexperienced lady-friends to a game, a special set of rules has been drawn up. These include the compulsory purchase of tickets in what is called the " Explaining Section," a block of seats set aside by the management for the purpose. The view of the diamond from this section is not very good, but it doesn't matter, as the men wouldn't see anything of the game anyway and the women can see just enough to give them material for questions and to whet their curiosity. As everyone around you is answering questions and trying to explain score-keeping, there is not the embarrassment which is usually attendant on being overheard by unattached fans in the vicinity. There is also not the distracting sound of breaking pencils and modified cursing to interfere with unattached fans' enjoyment of the game.

Absolutely no gentlemen with uninformed ladies will be admitted to the main stand. In order to enforce this regulation, a short examination on the rudiments of the game will take place at the gate, in which ladies will be expected to answer briefly the following questions: (Women examiners will be in attendance.)

1. What game is it that is being played on this field?

2. How many games have you seen before?

3. What is (a) a pitcher; (b) a base; (c) a bat?

4. What color uniform does the home-team wear?

5. What is the name of the home-team?

6. In the following sentence, cross out the incorrect statements, leaving the correct one: The catcher stands (1) directly behind the pitcher in the pitcher's box; (2) at the gate taking tickets; (3)

behind the batter; (4) at the bottom of the main aisle, selling ginger-ale.

7. What again is the name of the game you expect to see played?

8. Do you cry easily?

9. Is there anything else you would rather be doing this afternoon?

10. If so, please go and do it.

It has been decided that the American baseball fan should have a distinctive dress. A choice has been made from among the more popular styles and the following has been designated as regulation, embodying, as it does, the spirit and tone of the great national pastime.

Straw hat, worn well back on the head; one cigar, unlighted, held between teeth; coat held across knees; vest worn but unbuttoned and open, displaying both a belt and suspenders, with gold watch-chain connecting the bottom pockets.

The vest may be an added expense to certain fans who do not wear vests during the summer months, but it has been decided that it is absolutely essential to the complete costume, and no true baseball enthusiast will hesitate in complying.

VIII

HOW TO BE A SPECTATOR AT
SPRING PLANTING

THE danger in watching gardening, as in watching many other sports, is that you may be drawn into it yourself. This you must fight against. Your sinecure standing depends on a rigid abstinence from any of the work itself. Once you stoop over to hold one end of a string for a groaning planter, once you lift one shovelful of earth or toss out one stone, you become a worker and a worker is an abomination in the eyes of the true garden watcher.

A fence is, therefore, a great help. You may take up your position on the other side of the fence from the garden and lean heavily against it smoking a pipe, or you may even sit on it. Anything so long as you are out of helping distance and yet near enough so that the worker will be within easy range of your voice. You ought to be able to point a great deal, also.

There is much to be watched during the early stages of garden-preparation. Nothing is so satisfying as to lean ruminatingly against a fence and observe the slow, rhythmic swing of the digger's back or hear the repeated scraping of the shovel-edge against some buried rock. It sometimes is a help to the digger to sing a chanty, just to give him the beat. And then sometimes it is not. He will tell you in case he doesn't need it.

There is always a great deal for the watcher to do in the nature of comment on the soil. This is especially true if it is a new garden or has never been cultivated before by the present owner. The idea is to keep the owner from becoming too sanguine over the prospects.

" That soil looks pretty clayey," is a good thing to say. (It is hard to say, clearly, too. You had better practise it before trying it out on the gardener).

"I don't think that you'll have much luck with potatoes in that kind of earth," is another helpful approach. It is even better to go at it the other way, finding out first what the owner expects to plant. It may be that he isn't going to plant any potatoes, and then there you are, stuck with a perfectly dandy prediction which has no bearing on the case. It is time enough to pull it after he has told you that he expects to plant peas, beans, beets, corn. Then you can interrupt him and say: " Corn? " incredulously. " You don't expect to get any corn in that soil do you? Don't you know that corn requires a large percentage of bi-carbonate of soda in the soil, and I don't think, from the looks, that there is an ounce of soda bi-carb. in your whole plot. Even if the corn does come up, it will be so tough you can't eat it."

Then you can laugh, and call out to a neighbor, or even to the man's wife: " Hey, what do you know? Steve here thinks he's going to get some corn up in this soil! "

The watcher will find plenty to do when the time comes to pick the stones out of the freshly turned-over earth. It is his work to get upon a high place where he can survey the whole garden and detect the more obvious rocks.

" Here is a big fella over here, Steve," he may say. Or: " Just run your rake a little over in that corner. I'll bet you'll find a nest of them there."

" Plymouth Rock " is a funny thing to call any particularly offensive boulder, and is sure to get a laugh, especially if you kid the digger good-naturedly about being a Pilgrim and landing on it. He may even give it to you to keep.

Just as a matter of convenience for the worker, watchers have sometimes gone to the trouble of keeping count of the number of stones thrown out.

This is done by shouting out the count after each stone has been tossed. It makes a sort of game of the thing, and in this spirit the digger may be urged on to make a record.

" That's forty-eight, old man! Come on now, make her fifty. Attaboy, forty-nine! Only one more to go. We-want-fifty-we-want-fifty-we-want fifty."

And not only stones will be found, but queer objects which have got themselves buried in the ground during the winter-months and have become metamorphosed, so they are half way between one thing and another. As the digger holds one of these *objets dirt* gingerly between his thumb and forefinger the watcher has plenty of opportunity to shout out:

" You'd better save that. It may come in handy some day. What is it, Eddie? Your old beard? "

And funny cracks like that.

Here is where it is going to be difficult to keep to your resolution about not helping. After the digging, and stoning, and turning-over has been done, and the ground is all nice and soft and loamy, the idea of running a rake softly over the susceptible surface and leaving a beautiful even design in its wake, is almost too tempting to be withstood.

The worker himself will do all that he can to

"Atta boy, forty-nine: Only one more to go!"

make it hard for you. He will rake with evident delight, much longer than is necessary, back and forth, across and back, cocking his head and surveying the pattern and fixing it up along the edges with a care which is nothing short of insulting considering the fact that the whole thing has got to be mussed up again when the planting begins.

If you feel that you can no longer stand it without offering to assist, get down from the fence and go into your own house and up to your own room. There pray for strength. By the time you come down, the owner of the garden ought to have stopped raking and got started on the planting.

Here the watcher's task is almost entirely advisory. And, for the first part of the planting, he should lie low and say nothing. Wait until the planter has got his rows marked out and has wobbled along on his knees pressing the seeds into perhaps half the length of his first row. Then say:

"Hey there, Charlie! You've got those rows going the wrong way."

Charlie will say no he hasn't. Then he will ask what you mean the wrong way.

"Why, you poor cod, you've got them running north and south. They ought to go east and west. The sun rises over there, doesn't it?" (Charlie will attempt to deny this, but you must go right on.)

[45]

"And it comes on up behind that tree and over my roof and sets over there, doesn't it?" (By this time, Charlie will be crying with rage.) "Well, just as soon as your beans get up an inch or two they are going to cast a shadow right down the whole row and only those in front will ever get any sun. You can't grow things without sun, you know."

If Charlie takes you seriously and starts in to rearrange his rows in the other direction, you might perhaps get down off the fence and go in the house. You have done enough. If he doesn't take you seriously, you surely had better go in.

IX

THE MANHATTADOR

ANNOUNCEMENTS have been made of a
bull-fight to be held in Madison Square
Garden, New York, in which only the more humane
features of the Spanish institution are to be re-
tained. The bull will not be killed, or even hurt,
and horses will not be used as bait.

If a bull-fight must be held, this is of course the
way to hold it, but what features are to be sub-
stituted for the playful gorings and stabbings of
the Madrid system? Something must be done to
enrage the bull, otherwise he will just sulk in a
corner or walk out on the whole affair. Following
is a suggestion for the program of events:

1. Grand parade around the ring, headed by a
brass-band and the mayor in matador's costume.
Invitations to march in this parade will be issued
to every one in the bull-fighting set with the excep-
tion of the bull, who will be ignored. This will
make him pretty sore to start with.

2. After the marchers have been seated, the bull
will be led into the ring. An organized cheering

section among the spectators will immediately start jeering him, whistling, and calling " Take off those horns, we know you! "

3. The picadors will now enter, bearing pikes with ticklers on the ends. These will be brushed across the bull's nose as the picadors rush past him on noisy motor-cycles. The noise of the motor-cycles is counted on to irritate the bull quite as much as the ticklers, as he will probably be trying to sleep at the time.

4. Enter the bandilleros, carrying various ornate articles of girls' clothing (daisy-hat with blue ribbons, pink sash, lace jabot, etc.) which will, one by one, be hung on the bull when he isn't looking. In order to accomplish this, one of the bandilleros will engage the animal in conversation while another sneaks up behind him with the frippery. When he is quite trimmed, the bandilleros will withdraw to behind a shelter and call him: " Lizzie! "

5. By this time, the bull will be almost crying he will be so sore. This is the moment for the entrance of the intrepid matador. The matador will wear an outing cap with a cutaway and Jaeger vest, and the animal will become so infuriated by this inexcusable *mésalliance* of garments that he will charge madly at his antagonist. The matador, who will be equipped with boxing-gloves, will feint with

his left and pull the daisy-hat down over the bull's eyes with his right, immediately afterward stepping quickly to one side. The bull, blinded by the daisies, will not know where to go next and soon will laughingly admit that the joke has been on him. He will then allow the matador to jump on his back and ride around the ring, making good-natured attempts to unseat his rider.

X

WHAT TO DO WHILE THE FAMILY IS AWAY

SOMEWHERE or other the legend has sprung up that, as soon as the family goes away for the summer, Daddy brushes the hair over his bald spot, ties up his shoes, and goes out on a whirlwind trip through the hellish districts of town. The funny papers are responsible for this, just as they are responsible for the idea that all millionaires are fat and that Negroes are inordinately fond of watermelons.

I will not deny that for just about four minutes after the train has left, bearing Mother, Sister, Junior, Ingabog and the mechanical walrus on their way to Anybunkport, Daddy is suffused with a certain queer feeling of being eleven years old and down-town alone for the first time with fifteen cents to spend on anything he wants. The city seems to spread itself out before him just ablaze with lights and his feet rise lightly from the ground as if attached to toy balloons. I do not deny that his first move is to straighten his tie.

WHEN THE FAMILY IS AWAY

But five minutes would be a generous allowance for the duration of this foot-loose elation. As he leaves the station he suddenly becomes aware of the fact that no one else has heard about his being fancy-free. Everyone seems to be going somewhere in a very important manner. A great many people, oddly enough seem to be going home. Ordinarily he would be going home, too. But there would not be much sense in going home now, without ——. But come, come, this is no way to feel! Buck up, man! How about a wild oat or two?

Around at the club the doorman says that Mr. McNartly hasn't been in all afternoon and that Mr. Freem was in at about four-thirty but went out again with a bag. There is no one in the lounge whom he ever saw before. A lot of new members must have been taken in at the last meeting. The club is running down fast. He calls up Eddie Mastayer's office but he has gone for the day. Oh, well, someone will probably come in for dinner. He hasn't eaten dinner at the club for a long time and there will be just time for a swim before settling down to a nice piece of salmon steak.

All the new members seem to be congregated now in the pool and they look him over as if he were a fresh-air child being given a day's outing. He becomes self-conscious and slips on the marble floor, falling and hurting his shin quite badly. Who the hell are these people anyway? And where is the old bunch? He emerges from the locker room much hotter than he was before and in addition, boiling with rage.

Dinner is one of the most depressing rituals he has ever gone through with. Even the waiters seem unfamiliar. Once he even gets up and goes out to the front of the building to see if he hasn't got into the wrong club-house by mistake. Pretty soon a terrible person whose name is either Riegle or Ropple comes and sits down with him, offering as his share of the conversation the dogmatic announcement that it has been hotter today than it was yesterday. This is denied with some feeling, although it is known to be true. Dessert is dispensed with for the sake of getting away from Riegle or Ropple or whatever his name is.

Then the first gay evening looms up ahead. What to do? There is nothing to prevent his drawing all the money out of the bank and tearing the town wide open from the City Hall to the Soldier's Monument. There is nothing to prevent his formally introducing himself to some nice blonde and watching her get the meat out of a lobster-claw. There is nothing to prevent his hiring some boot-

WHEN THE FAMILY IS AWAY

legger to anoint him with synthetic gin until he
glows like a fire-fly and imagines that he has just
been elected Mayor on a Free Ice-Cream ticket.
Absolutely nothing stands in his way, except a dis-
pairing vision of crêpe letters before his eyes reading: " — And For What? "

He ends up by going to the movies where he falls
asleep. Rather than go home to the empty house
he stays at the club. In the morning he is at the
office at a quarter to seven.

Now there ought to be several things that a man
could do at home to relieve the tedium of his existence while the family is away. Once you get
accustomed to the sound of your footsteps on the
floors and reach a state of self-control where you
don't break down and sob every time you run into
a toy which has been left standing around, there are
lots of ways of keeping yourself amused in an
empty house.

You can set the victrola going and dance. You
may never have had an opportunity to get off by
yourself and practice those new steps without someone's coming suddenly into the room and making
you look foolish. (That's one big advantage about
being absolutely alone in a house. You can't *look*
foolish, no matter what you do. You may *be*
foolish, but no one except you and your God knows

[53]

about it and God probably has a great deal too much to do to go around telling people how foolish you were). So roll back the rugs and put on " Kalua " and, holding out one arm in as fancy a manner as you wish, slip the other daintily about the waist of an imaginary partner and step out. You'd be surprised to see how graceful you are. Pretty soon you will get confidence to try a few tricks. A very nice one is to stop in the middle of a step, point the left toe delicately twice in time to the music, dip, and whirl. It makes no difference if you fall on the whirl. Who cares? And when you are through dancing you can go out to the faucet and get yourself a drink — provided the water hasn't been turned off.

Lots of fun may also be had by going out into the kitchen and making things with whatever is left in the pantry. There will probably be plenty of salt and nutmegs, with boxes of cooking soda, tapioca, corn-starch and maybe, if you are lucky, an old bottle of olives. Get out a cook-book and choose something that looks nice in the picture. In place of the ingredients which you do not have, substitute those which you do, thus: nutmegs for eggs, tapioca for truffles, corn-starch and water for milk, and so forth and so forth. Then go in and set the table according to the instructions in the cook-book for a Washington's Birthday party, light the candles, and with one of them set fire to the house.

There is probably a night-train for Anybunkport which you can catch while the place is still burning.

. . . .

To those male readers whose families are away for the summer:

Tear the above story out along dotted line and mail it to the folks, writing in pencil across the top " This guy has struck it about right." Then drop around tonight at seven-thirty to Eddie's apartment. Joe Reddish, John Liftwich, Harry Thibault and three others will be there and the limit will be fifty cents. Game will absolutely *break up at one-thirty. No fooling. One-thirty and not a minute longer.*

XI

" ROLL YOUR OWN "

*Inside Points on Building and Maintaining a
Private Tennis Court*

NOW that the Great War is practically over,
until the next one begins there isn't very
much that you can do with that large plot of
ground which used to be your war-garden. It is
too small for a running-track and too large for
nasturtiums. Obviously, the only thing left is a
tennis-court.

One really ought to have a tennis-court of one's
own. Those at the Club are always so full that on
Saturdays and Sundays the people waiting to play
look like the gallery at a Davis Cup match, and
even when you do get located you have two sets of
balls to chase, yours and those of the people in the
next court.

The first thing is to decide among yourselves just
what kind of court it is to be. There are three
kinds: grass, clay, and corn-meal. In Maine,
gravel courts are also very popular. Father will
usually hold out for a grass court because it gives

a slower bounce to the ball and Father isn't so quick on the bounce as he used to be. All Mother insists on is plenty of headroom. Junior and Myrtis will want a clay one because you can dance on a clay one in the evening. The court as finished will be a combination grass and dirt, with a little golden-rod late in August.

A little study will be necessary before laying out the court. I mean you can't just go out and mark a court by guess-work. You must first learn what the dimensions are supposed to be and get as near to them as is humanly possible. Whereas there might be a slight margin for error in some measure-ments, it is absolutely essential that both sides are the same length, otherwise you might end up by lobbing back to yourself if you got very excited.

The worst place to get the dope on how to arrange a tennis-court is in the Encyclopædia Bri-tannica. The article on TENNIS was evidently written by the Archbishop of Canterbury. It be-gins by explaining that in America tennis is called " court tennis." The only answer to that is, " You're a cock-eyed liar! " The whole article is like this.

The name " tennis," it says, probably comes from the French " *Tenez!* " meaning " Take it! Play! " More likely, in my opinion, it is derived from the

LOVE CONQUERS ALL

Polish " *Tinith!* " meaning " Go on, that was *not* outside! "

During the Fourteenth Century the game was played by the highest people in France. Louis X died from a chill contracted after playing. Charles V was devoted to it, although he tried in vain to stop it as a pastime for the lower classes (the origin of the country-club); Charles VI watched it being played from the room where he was confined during his attack of insanity and Du Guesclin amused himself with it during the siege of Dinan. And, although it doesn't say so in the Encyclopædia, Robert C. Benchley, after playing for the first time in the season of 1922, was so lame under the right shoulder-blade that he couldn't lift a glass to his mouth.

This fascinating historical survey of tennis goes on to say that in the reign of Henri IV the game was so popular that it was said that " there were more tennis-players in Paris than drunkards in England." The drunkards of England were so upset by this boast that they immediately started a drive for membership with the slogan, " Five thousand more drunkards by April 15, and to Hell with France! " One thing led to another until war was declared.

The net does not appear until the 17th century.

Up until that time a rope, either fringed or tasseled, was stretched across the court. This probably had to be abandoned because it was so easy to crawl under it and chase your opponent. There might also have been ample opportunity for the person playing at the net or at the " rope," to catch the eye of the player directly opposite by waving his racquet high in the air and then to kick him under the rope, knocking him for a loop while the ball was being put into play in his territory. You have to watch these Frenchmen every minute.

The Encyclopædia Britannica gives fifteen lines to " Tennis in America." It says that " few tennis courts existed in America before 1880, but that now there are courts in Boston, New York, Chicago, Tuxedo and Lakewood and several other places." Everyone try hard to think now just where those other places are!

Which reminds us that one of them is going to be in your side yard where the garden used to be. After you have got the dimensions from the Encyclopædia, call up a professional tennis-court maker and get him to do the job for you. Just tell him that you want " a tennis-court."

Once it is built the fun begins. According to the arrangement, each member of the family is to have certain hours during which it belongs to them and

no one else. Thus the children can play before
breakfast and after breakfast until the sun gets
around so that the west court is shady. Then
Daddy and Mother and sprightly friends may take
it over. Later in the afternoon the children have it
again, and if there is any light left after dinner
Daddy can take a whirl at the ball.

What actually will happen is this: Right after
breakfast Roger Beeman, who lives across the street
and who is home for the summer with a couple of
college friends who are just dandy looking, will
come over and ask if they may use the court until
someone wants it. They will let Myrtis play with
them and perhaps Myrtis' girl-chum from Westover. They will play five sets, running into scores
like 19-17, and at lunch time will make plans for a
ride into the country for the afternoon. Daddy will
stick around in the offing all dressed up in his
tennis-clothes waiting to play with Uncle Ted, but
somehow or other every time he approaches the
court the young people will be in the middle of a set.

After lunch, Lillian Nieman, who lives three
houses down the street, will come up and ask if she
may bring her cousin (just on from the West) to
play a set until someone wants the court. Lillian's
cousin has never played tennis before but she has
done a lot of croquet and thinks she ought to pick

For three hours there is a great deal of screaming.

tennis up rather easily. For three hours there is a great deal of screaming, with Lillian and her cousin hitting the ball an aggregate of eleven times, while Daddy patters up and down the side-lines, all dressed up in white, practising shots against the netting.

Finally, the girls will ask him to play with them, and he will thank them and say that he has to go in the house now as he is all perspiration and is afraid of catching cold.

After dinner there is dancing on the court by the young people. Anyway, Daddy is getting pretty old for tennis.

XII

DO INSECTS THINK?

IN a recent book entitled, " The Psychic Life of Insects," Professor Bouvier says that we must be careful not to credit the little winged fellows with intelligence when they behave in what seems like an intelligent manner. They may be only reacting. I would like to confront the Professor with an instance of reasoning power on the part of an insect which can not be explained away in any such manner.

During the summer of 1899, while I was at work on my treatise " Do Larvae Laugh," we kept a female wasp at our cottage in the Adirondacks. It really was more like a child of our own than a wasp, except that it *looked* more like a wasp than a child of our own. That was one of the ways we told the difference.

It was still a young wasp when we got it (thirteen or fourteen years old) and for some time we could not get it to eat or drink, it was so shy. Since it was a, female, we decided to call it Miriam, but soon the children's nickname for it — " Pudge " — became a fixture, and " Pudge " it was from that time on.

One evening I had been working late in my laboratory fooling round with some gin and other chemicals, and in leaving the room I tripped over a nine of diamonds which someone had left lying on the floor and knocked over my card catalogue containing the names and addresses of all the larvae worth knowing in North America. The cards went everywhere.

I was too tired to stop to pick them up that night, and went sobbing to bed, just as mad as I could be. As I went, however, I noticed the wasp flying about in circles over the scattered cards. " Maybe Pudge will pick them up," I said half-laughingly to myself, never thinking for one moment that such would be the case.

When I came down the next morning Pudge was still asleep over in her box, evidently tired out. And well she might have been. For there on the floor lay the cards scattered all about just as I had left them the night before. The faithful little insect had buzzed about all night trying to come to some decision about picking them up and arranging them in the catalogue-box, and then, figuring out for herself that, as she knew practically nothing about larvae of any sort except wasp-larvae, she would probably make more of a mess of rearranging them than as if she left them on the floor for me to fix. It was just too much for her to tackle, and, discouraged, she went over and lay down in her box, where she cried herself to sleep.

If this is not an answer to Professor Bouvier's statement that insects have no reasoning power, I do not know what is.

XIII

THE SCORE IN THE STANDS

THE opening week of the baseball season brought out few surprises. The line-up in the grandstands was practically the same as when the season closed last Fall, most of the fans busying themselves before the first game started by picking old 1921 seat checks and October peanut crumbs out of the pockets of their light-weight overcoats.

Old-timers on the two teams recognized the familiar faces in the bleachers and were quick to give them a welcoming cheer. The game by innings as it was conducted by the spectators is as follows:

FIRST INNING: Scanlon, sitting in the first-base bleachers, yelled to Ruth to lead off with a homer. Thibbets sharpened his pencil. Liebman and O'Rourke, in the south stand, engaged in a bitter controversy over Peckingpaugh's last-season batting average. NO RUNS.

SECOND INNING: Scanlon yelled to Bodie to to whang out a double. Turtelot said that Bodie couldn't do it. Scanlon said " Oh, is that so? " Turtelot said " Yes, that's so and whad' yer know

[65]

LOVE CONQUERS ALL

about that?" Bodie whanged out a double and
Scanlon's collar came undone and he lost his
derby. Stevens announced that this made Bodie's
batting average 1000 for the season so far. Joslin
laughed.

THIRD INNING: Thibbets sharpened his pencil. Zinnzer yelled to Mays to watch out for a fast
one. Steinway yelled to Mays to watch out for a
slow one. Mays fanned. O'Rourke called out and
asked Brazill how all the little brazil-nuts were.
Levy turned to O'Rourke and said he'd brazil-nut
him. O'Rourke said "Eah? When do you start
doing it?" Levy said: "Right now." O'Rourke
said: "All right, come on. I'm waiting." Levy
said: "Eah?" O'Rourke said: "Well, why don't
you come, you big haddock?" Levy said he'd wait
for O'Rourke outside where there weren't any ladies. NO RUNS.

FOURTH INNING: Scanlon called out to Ruth
to knock a homer. Thibbets sharpened his pencil.
Scanlon yelled: "Atta-boy, Babe, whad' I tell
yer!" when Ruth got a single.

FIFTH INNING: Mrs. Whitebait asked Mr.
Whitebait how you marked a home-run on the
score-card. Mr. Whitebait said: "Why do you
have to know? No one has knocked a home-run."
Mrs. Whitebait said that Babe Ruth ran home in

[66]

the last inning. " Yes, I know," said Mr. White-bait, " but it wasn't a home-run." Mrs. W. asked him with some asperity just why it wasn't a home-run, if a man ran home, especially if it was Babe Ruth. Mr. W. said: " I'll tell you later. I want to watch the game." Mrs. Whitebait began to cry a little. Mr. Whitebait groaned and snatched the card away from her and marked a home-run for Ruth in the fourth inning.

SIXTH INNING: Thurston called out to Hasty not to let them fool him. Wicker said that where Hasty got fooled in the first place was when he let them tell him he could play baseball. Unknown man said that he was " too Hasty," and laughed very hard. Thurston said that Hasty was a better pitcher than Mays, when he was in form. Unknown man said " Eah? " and laughed very hard again. Wicker asked how many times in seven years Hasty was in form and Thurston replied: " Often enough for you." Unknown man said that what Hasty needed was some hasty-pudding, and laughed so hard that his friend had to take him out.

Thibbets sharpened his pencil.

SEVENTH INNING: Libby called " Every-body up! " as if he had just originated the idea, and seemed proudly pleased when everyone stood up. Taussig threw money to the boy for a bag of

peanuts who tossed the bag to Levy who kept it.
Taussig to boy to Levy.

Scanlon yelled to Ruth to come through with a
homer. Ruth knocked a single and Scanlon yelled
" Atta-boy, Babe! All-er way 'round! All-er way
round, Babe! " Mrs. Whitebait asked Mr. Whitebait which were the Clevelands. Mr. Whitebait said
very quietly that the Clevelands weren't playing today, just New York and Philadelphia and that only
two teams could play the game at the same time, that
perhaps next year they would have it so that Cleve-
land and Philadelphia could both play New York at
once but the rules would have to be changed first.
Mrs. Whitebait said that he didn't have to be so
nasty about is. Mr. W. said My God, who's being
nasty? Mrs. W. said that the only reason she came
up with him anyway to see the Giants play was because then she knew that he wasn't off with a lot of
bootleggers. Mr. W. said that it wasn't the Giants
but the Yankees that she was watching and where
did she get that bootlegger stuff. Mrs. W. said never
mind where she got it. NO RUNS.

EIGHTH INNING: Thibbets sharpened his
pencil. Litner got up and went home. Scanlon
yelled to Ruth to end up the game with a homer.
Ruth singled. Scanlon yelled " Atta-Babe! " and
went home.

THE SCORE IN THE STANDS

NINTH INNING: Stevens began figuring up the players' batting averages for the season thus far. Wicker called over to Thurston and asked him how Mr. Hasty was now. Thurston said "That's all right how he is." Mrs. Whitebait said that she intended to go to her sister's for dinner and that Mr. Whitebait could do as he liked. Mr. Whitebait told her to bet that he would do just that. Thibbets broke his pencil.

Score: New York 11. Philadelphia 1

XIV

MID–WINTER SPORTS

THESE are melancholy days for the newspaper sporting-writers. The complaints are
all in from old grads of Miami who feel that there
weren't enough Miami men on the All-American
football team, and it is too early to begin writing
about the baseball training camps. Once in a while
some lady swimmer goes around a tank three hundred times, or the holder of the Class B squash
championship " meets all-comers in court tilt," but
aside from that, the sporting world is buried with
the nuts for the winter.

Since sporting-writers must live, why not intro-
duce a few items of general interest into their columns, accounts of the numerous contests of speed
and endurance which take place during the winter
months in the homes of our citizenry? For instance:

The nightly races between Mr. and Mrs. Theodore
M. Twamly, to see who can get into bed first, leaving the opening of the windows and putting out of
the light for the loser, was won last night for the

first time this winter by Mr. Twamly. Strategy entered largely into the victory, Mr. Twamly getting into bed with most of his clothes on.

An interesting exhibition of endurance was given by Martin W. Lasbert at his home last evening when he covered the distance between the cold-water tap in his bath-room to the bedside of his young daughter, Mertice, eighteen times in three hours, this being the number of her demands for water to drink. When interviewed after the eighteenth lap, Mr. Lasbert said: " I wouldn't do it another time, not if the child were parching." Shortly after that he made his nineteenth trip.

As was exclusively predicted in these columns yesterday and in accordance with all the dope, Chester H. Flerlie suffered his sixtieth consecutive defeat last evening at the hands of the American Radiator Company, the builders of his furnace. With all respect for Mr. Flerlie's pluck in attempting, night after night, to dislodge clinkers caught in the grate, it must be admitted, even by his host of friends, that he might much better be engaged in some gainful occupation. The grate tackled by the doughty challenger last night was one of the fine-tooth comb variety (the " Non-Sifto " No.

114863), in which the clinker is caught by a patent clutch and held securely until the wrecking-crew arrives. At the end of the bout Mr. Flerlie was led away to his dressing room, suffering from lacerated hands and internal injuries. "I'm through," was his only comment.

This morning's winners in the Lymedale commuters' contest for seats on the shady side of the car on the 8:28 were L. Y. Irman, Sydney M. Gissith, John F. Nothman and Louis Leque. All the other seats were won by commuters from Loose Valley, the next station above Lymedale. In trying to scramble up the car-steps in advance of lady passengers, Merton Steef had his right shin badly skinned and hit his jaw on the bottom step. Time was *not* called while his injuries were being looked after.

Before an enthusiastic and notable gathering, young Lester J. Dimmik, age three, put to rout his younger brother, Carl Withney Dimmik, Jr., age two, in their matutinal contest to see which can dispose of his Wheatena first. In the early stages of the match, it began to look as if the bantamweight would win in a walk, owing to his trick of throwing spoonfuls of the breakfast food over his shoulder

[72]

He was further aided by the breaks of the game.

and under the tray of his high-chair. The referees soon put a stop to this, however, and specified that the Wheatena must be placed *in* the mouth. This cramped Dimmick Junior's form and it soon became impossible for him to locate his mouth at all. At this point, young Lester took the lead, which he maintained until he crossed the line an easy winner. As a reward he was relieved of the necessity of eating another dish of Wheatena.

Stephen L. Agnew was the lucky guest in the home of Orrin F. McNeal this week-end, beating out Lee Stable for first chance at the bath-tub on Sunday morning. Both contestants came out of their bed rooms at the same time, but Agnew's room being nearer the bath-room, he made the distance down the hall in two seconds quicker time than his somewhat heavier opponent, and was further aided by the breaks of the game when Stable dropped his sponge half-way down the straightaway. Agnew's time in the bath-room was 1 hr. and 25 minutes.

XV

READING THE FUNNIES ALOUD

ONE of the minor enjoyable features of having children is the necessity of reading aloud to them the colored comic sections in the Sunday papers.

And no matter how good your intentions may have been at first to keep the things out of the house (the comic sections, not the children) sooner or later there comes a Sunday when you find that your little boy has, in some underground fashion, learned of the raucous existence of *Simon Simp* or the *Breakback Babies,* and is demanding the current installment with a fervor which will not be denied.

Sunday morning in our house has now become a time for low subterfuge on the part of Doris and me in our attempts to be somewhere else when Junior appears dragging the " funnies " (a loathsome term in itself) to be read to him. I make believe that the furnace looks as if it might fall apart at any minute if it is not watched closely, and Doris calls from upstairs that she may be some time over the weekly accounts.

[74]

READING THE FUNNIES ALOUD

But sooner or later Junior ferrets one of us out and presents himself beaming. "*Now* will you read me the 'funnies'?" is the dread sentence which opens the siege. It then becomes a rather ill-natured contest between Doris and me to see which can pick the more bearable pages to read, leaving the interminable ones, containing great balloons pregnant with words, for the other.

I usually find that Doris has read the Briggs page to Junior before I get downstairs, the Briggs page (and possibly the drawings of Voight's *Lester De Pester*) being the only department that an adult mind can dwell on and keep its self-respect. " Now *I* will read you Briggs," says Doris with the air of an indulgent parent, but settling down with great relish to the task, " and Daddy will read you the others."

Having been stuck for over a year with " the others " I have now reached a stage where I utilize a sort of second sight in the reading whereby the words are seen and pronounced without ever registering on my brain at all. And, as I sit with Junior impassive on my lap (just why children should so frantically seek to have the " funnies " read to them is a mystery, for they never by any chance seem to derive the slightest emotional pleasure from the recital but sit in stony silence as if they rather disapproved of the whole thing after all) I have evolved a system which enables me to carry on a little constructive thinking while reading aloud, thereby keeping the time from being entirely wasted. Heaven knows we get little enough opportunity to sit down and think things out in this busy work-a-day world, so that this little period of mental freedom is in the nature of a godsend. Thus:

What Is Being Read Aloud	*Concurrent Thinking*
" Here he says ' Gee but this is tough luck a new automobile an' no place to go ' and the dog is saying ' It aint so tough at that ' Then here in the next picture the old man says ' Percy ain't in my class as a chauffeur, he ain't as fearless as me ' and this one is saying ' Hello there, that looks like the old tin Lizzie that I gave to the General last year I guess I'll take a peek and see what's up ' ' Well what are you doing hanging around here, what do you think this is a hotel ? ' ' Say where do you get that stuff you ain't no justice of the peace you know ' ' Wow! Let me out let me out, I say ' ' I'll show you biff biff wham zowie! ' etc. etc. "	" Here I am in the thirties and it is high time that I made something of myself. Is my job as good as I deserve ? By studying nights I might fit myself for a better position in the foreign exchange department, but that would mean an outlay of money. Furthermore, is it, on the whole, wise to attempt to hurry the workings of Fate ? Is not perhaps the determinist right who says that what we are and what we ever can be is already written in the books, that we can not alter the workings of Destiny one iota ? This theory is, of course, tenable, but, on the whole, it seems to me that if I were to take the matter into my own hands, etc. etc."

And then, when the last pot of boiling water has been upset over the last grandfather's back, and Junior has slid down from your lap as near satisfied as he ever will be, you have ten or fifteen minutes of constructive thinking behind you, which, if practiced every Sunday, will make you President of the company within a few years.

XVI

OPERA SYNOPSES

Some Sample Outlines of Grand Opera Plots For Home Study.

I

DIE MEISTER–GENOSSENSCHAFT

SCENE: *The Forests of Germany.*
TIME: *Antiquity.*

CAST

STRUDEL, *God of Rain*...................Basso
SCHMALZ, *God of Slight Drizzle*..........Tenor
IMMERGLÜCK, *Goddess of the Six Primary Colors* ....Soprano
LUDWIG DAS EIWEISS, *the Knight of the Iron Duck* ....Baritone
THE WOODPECKER....................Soprano

ARGUMENT

The basis of " Die Meister-Genossenschaft " is an old legend of Germany which tells how the Whale got his Stomach.

OPERA SYNOPSES

ACT 1

The Rhine at Low Tide Just Below Weld-schnoffen.—Immerglück has grown weary of always sitting on the same rock with the same fishes swimming by every day, and sends for Schwül to suggest something to do. Schwül asks her how she would like to have pass before her all the wonders of the world fashioned by the hand of man. She says, rotten. He then suggests that Ringblattz, son of Pflucht, be made to appear before her and fight a mortal combat with the Iron Duck. This pleases Immerglück and she summons to her the four dwarfs: Hot Water, Cold Water, Cool, and Cloudy. She bids them bring Ringblattz to her. They refuse, because Pflucht has at one time rescued them from being buried alive by acorns, and, in a rage, Immerglück strikes them all dead with a thunderbolt.

ACT 2

A Mountain Pass.—Repenting of her deed, Immerglück has sought advice of the giants, Offen and Besitz, and they tell her that she must procure the magic zither which confers upon its owner the power to go to sleep while apparently carrying on a conversation. This magic zither has been hidden for three hundred centuries in an old bureau drawer, guarded by the Iron Duck, and, although many have attempted to rescue it, all have died of a strange ailment just as success was within their grasp.

But Immerglück calls to her side Dampfboot, the tinsmith of the gods, and bids him make for her a tarnhelm or invisible cap which will enable her to talk to people without their understanding a word she says. For a dollar and a half extra Dampfboot throws in a magic ring which renders its wearer insensible. Thus armed, Immerglück starts out for Walhalla, humming to herself.

Act 3

The Forest Before the Iron Duck's Bureau Drawer.—Merglitz, who has up till this time held his peace, now descends from a balloon and demands the release of Betty. It has been the will of Wotan that Merglitz and Betty should meet on earth and hate each other like poison, but Zweiback, the druggist of the gods, has disobeyed and concocted a love-potion which has rendered the young couple very unpleasant company. Wotan, enraged, destroys them with a protracted heat spell.

Encouraged by this sudden turn of affairs, Immerglück comes to earth in a boat drawn by four white

Holsteins, and, seated alone on a rock, remembers aloud to herself the days when she was a girl. Pilgrims from Augenblick, on their way to worship at the shrine of Schmürr, hear the sound of reminiscence coming from the rock and stop in their march to sing a hymn of praise for the drying up of the crops. They do not recognize Immerglück, as she has her hair done differently, and think that she is a beggar girl selling pencils.

In the meantime, Ragel, the papercutter of the gods, has fashioned himself a sword on the forge of Schmalz, and has called the weapon " Assistance-in-Emergency." Armed with "Assistance-in-Emergency " he comes to earth, determined to slay the Iron Duck and carry off the beautiful Irma.

But Frimsel overhears the plan and has a drink brewed which is given to Ragel in a golden goblet and which, when drunk, makes him forget his past and causes him to believe that he is Schnorr, the God of Fun. While laboring under this spell, Ragel has a funeral pyre built on the summit of a high mountain and, after lighting it, climbs on top of it with a mandolin which he plays until he is consumed.

Immerglück never marries.

LOVE CONQUERS ALL

II

IL MINNESTRONE

(Peasant Love)

Scene: *Venice and Old Point Comfort.*
Time: *Early 16th Century.*

Cast

Alfonso, *Duke of Minnestrone*.........Baritone
Partola, *a Peasant Girl*...............Soprano
Cleanso ⎫   ⎧ Tenor
Turino ⎬ *Young Noblemen of Venice.* ⎨ Tenor
Bombo   ⎭   ⎩ Basso
Ludovico ⎱ *Assassins in the service of* ⎰   Basso
Astolfo ⎰   *Cafeteria Rusticana*   ⎱ Methodist
Townspeople, Cabbies and Sparrows

Argument

" Il Minnestrone " is an allegory of the two sides
of a man's nature (good and bad), ending at last
in an awfully comical mess with everyone dead.

Act i

A Public Square, Ferrara. — During a peasant
festival held to celebrate the sixth consecutive day
of rain, Rudolpho, a young nobleman, sees Lilliano,

daughter of the village bell-ringer, dancing along throwing artificial roses at herself. He asks of his secretary who the young woman is, and his secretary, in order to confuse Rudolpho and thereby win the hand of his ward, tells him that it is his (Rudolpho's) own mother, disguised for the festival. Rudolpho is astounded. He orders her arrest.

Act 2

Banquet Hall in Gorgio's Palace. — Lilliano has not forgotten Breda, her old nurse, in spite of her troubles, and determines to avenge herself for the many insults she received in her youth by poisoning her (Breda). She therefore invites the old nurse to a banquet and poisons her. Presently a knock is heard. It is Ugolfo. He has come to carry away the body of Michelo and to leave an extra quart of pasteurized. Lilliano tells him that she no longer loves him, at which he goes away, dragging his feet sulkily.

Act 3

In Front of Emilo's House. — Still thinking of the old man's curse, Borsa has an interview with Cleanso, believing him to be the Duke's wife. He tells him things can't go on as they are, and Cleanso stabs him. Just at this moment Betty comes rushing in from school and falls in a faint. Her worst fears have been realized. She has been insulted by Sigmundo, and presently dies of old age. In a fury, Ugolfo rushes out to kill Sigmundo and, as he does so, the dying Rosenblatt rises on one elbow and curses his mother.

III

LUCY DE LIMA

SCENE: *Wales.*
TIME: *1700 (Greenwich).*

CAST

WILLIAM WONT, *Lord of Glennnn* . . . . Basso
LUCY WAGSTAFF, *his daughter* . . . . Soprano
BERTRAM, *her lover* . . . . Tenor
LORD ROGER, *friend of Bertram* . . . . Soprano
IRMA, *attendant to Lucy* . . . . Basso

Friends, Retainers and Members of the local Lodge of Elks.

ARGUMENT

"Lucy de Lima," is founded on the well-known story by Boccaccio of the same name and address.

OPERA SYNOPSES

ACT 1

Gypsy Camp Near Waterbury. — The gypsies, led by Edith, go singing through the camp on the way to the fair. Following them comes Despard, the gypsy leader, carrying Ethel, whom he has just kidnapped from her father, who had previously just kidnapped her from her mother. Despard places Ethel on the ground and tells Mona, the old hag, to watch over her. Mona nurses a secret grudge against Despard for having once cut off her leg and decides to change Ethel for Nettie, another kidnapped child. Ethel pleads with Mona to let her stay with Despard, for she has fallen in love with him on the ride over. But Mona is obdurate.

ACT 2

The Fair. — A crowd of sightseers and villagers is present. Roger appears, looking for Laura. He can not find her. Laura appears, looking for Roger. She can not find him. The gypsy queen approaches Roger and thrusts into his hand the locket stolen from Lord Brym. Roger looks at it and is frozen with astonishment, for it contains the portrait of his mother when she was in high school. He then realizes that Laura must be his sister, and starts out to find her.

LOVE CONQUERS ALL

Act 3

Hall in the Castle. — Lucy is seen surrounded by every luxury, but her heart is sad. She has just been shown a forged letter from Stewart saying that he no longer loves her, and she remembers her old free life in the mountains and longs for another romp with Ravensbane and Wolfshead, her old pair of rompers. The guests begin to assemble for the wedding, each bringing a roast ox. They chide Lucy for not having her dress changed. Just at this moment the gypsy band bursts in and Cleon tells the wedding party that Elsie and not Edith is the child who was stolen from the summer-house, showing the blood-stained derby as proof. At this, Lord Brym repents and gives his blessing on the pair, while the fishermen and their wives celebrate in the courtyard.

XVII

THE YOUNG IDEA'S SHOOTING GALLERY

SINCE we were determined to have Junior educated according to modern methods of child training, a year and a half did not seem too early an age at which to begin. As Doris said: " There is no reason why a child of a year and a half shouldn't have rudimentary cravings for self-expression." And really, there isn't any reason, when you come right down to it.

Doris had been reading books on the subject, and had been talking with Mrs. Deemster. Most of the trouble in our town can be traced back to some-one's having been talking with Mrs. Deemster. Mrs. Deemster brings an evangelical note into the simplest social conversations, so that by the time your wife is through the second piece of cinnamon toast she is convinced that all children should have their knee-pants removed before they are four, or that you should hire four servants a day on three-hour shifts, or that, as in the present case, no child should be sent to a regular school until he has determined for himself what his profession is going to be and then should be sent straight from the home to Johns Hopkins or the Sorbonne.

Junior was to be left entirely to himself, the theory being that he would find self-expression in some form or other, and that by watching him carefully it could be determined just what should be developed in him, or, rather, just what he should be allowed to develop in himself. He was not to be corrected in any way, or guided, and he was to call us " Doris " and " Monty " instead of " Mother " and " Father." We were to be just pals, nothing more. Otherwise, his individuality would become submerged. I was, however, to be allowed to pay what few bills he might incur until he should find himself.

The first month that Junior was " on his own," striving for self-expression, he spent practically every waking hour of each day in picking the mortar out from between the bricks in the fire-place and eating it.

" Don't you think you ought to suggest to him that nobody who really *is* anybody eats mortar? " I said.

" I don't like to interfere," replied Doris. " I'm trying to figure out what it may mean. He may have the makings of a sculptor in him." But one could see that she was a little worried, so I didn't say the cheap and obvious thing, that at any rate he had the makings of a sculpture in him or would have in a few more days of self-expression.

Soft putty was put at his disposal, in case he might feel like doing a little modeling. We didn't expect much of him at first, of course; maybe just a panther or a little General Sherman; but if that was to be his *métier* we weren't going to have it said that his career was nipped in the bud for the lack of a little putty.

The first thing that he did was to stop up the keyhole in the bath-room door while I was in the tub, so that I had to crawl out on the piazza roof and into the guest-room window. It did seem as if there might be some way of preventing a recurrence of that sort of thing without submerging his individuality too much. But Doris said no. If he were disciplined now, he would grow up nursing a complex against putty and against me and might even try to marry Aunt Marian. She had read of a little boy who had been punished by his father for putting soap on the cellar stairs, and from that time on, all the rest of his life, every time he saw soap he went to bed and dreamed that he was riding in the cab of a runaway engine dressed as Perriot, which meant, of course, that he had a suppressed desire to kill his father.

It almost seemed, however, as if the risk were worth taking if Junior could be shown the fundamentally anti-social nature of an act like stuffing keyholes with putty, but nothing was done about it except to take the putty supply away for that day. The chief trouble came, however, in Junior's contacts with other neighborhood children whose parents had not seen the light. When Junior would lead a movement among the young bloods to pull up the Hemmings' nasturtiums or would show flashes of personality by hitting little Leda Hemming over the forehead with a trowel, Mrs. Hemming could never be made to see that to reprimand Junior would be to crush out his God-given individuality. All she would say was, " Just look at those nasturtiums! " over and over again. And the Hemming children were given to understand that it would be all right if they didn't play with Junior quite so much.

This morning, however, the thing solved itself. While expressing himself in putty in the nursery, Junior succeeded in making a really excellent life-mask of Mrs. Deemster's fourteen-months-old little

Mrs. Deemster didn't enter into the spirit of the thing at all.

girl who had come over to spend the morning with him. She had a little difficulty in breathing, but it really was a fine mask. Mrs. Deemster, however, didn't enter into the spirit of the thing at all, and after excavating her little girl, took Doris aside. It was decided that Junior is perhaps too young to start in on his career unguided.

That is Junior that you can hear now, I think.

XVIII

POLYP WITH A PAST

THE STORY OF AN ORGANISM WITH A HEART

O F all forms of animal life, the polyp is probably the most neglected by fanciers. People
seem willing to pay attention to anything, cats,
lizards, canaries, or even fish, but simply because
the polyp is reserved by nature and not given to
showing off or wearing its heart on its sleeve, it is
left alone under the sea to slave away at coral-
building with never a kind word or a pat on the
tentacles from anybody.

It was quite by accident that I was brought face
to face with the human side of a polyp. I had
been working on a thesis on " Emotional Crises in
Sponge Life," and came upon a polyp formation on
a piece of coral in the course of my laboratory work.
To say that I was astounded would be putting it
mildly. I was surprised.

The difficulty in research work in this field came
in isolating a single polyp from the rest in order
to study the personal peculiarities of the little organism, for, as is so often the case (even, I fear, with

us great big humans sometimes), the individual
behaves in an entirely different manner in private
from the one he adopts when there is a crowd around.
And a polyp, among all creatures, has a minimum of
time to himself in which to sit down and think.
There is always a crowd of other polyps dropping
in on him, urging him to make a fourth in a string
of coral beads or just to come out and stick around
on a rock for the sake of good-fellowship.

The one which I finally succeeded in isolating
was an engaging organism with a provocative manner
and a little way of wrinkling up its ectoderm which
put you at once at your ease. There could be no
formality about your relations with this polyp five
minutes after your first meeting. You were just
like one great big family.

Although I have no desire to retail gossip, I think
that readers of this treatise ought to be made aware
of the fact (if, indeed, they do not already know
it) that a polyp is really neither one thing nor
another in matters of gender. One day it may be
a little boy polyp, another day a little girl, according to its whim or practical considerations of policy.
On gray days, when everything seems to be going
wrong, it may decide that it will be neither boy nor
girl but will just drift. I think that if we big
human cousins of the little polyp were to follow

the example set by these lowliest of God's creatures in this matter, we all would find ourselves much better off in the end. Am I not right, little polyp?

What was my surprise, then, to discover my little friend one day in a gloomy and morose mood. It refused the peanut-butter which I had brought it and I observed through the microscope that it was shaking with sobs. Lifting it up with a pair of pincers I took it over to the window to let it watch the automobiles go by, a diversion which had, in the past, never failed to amuse. But I could see that it was not interested. A tune from the victrola fell equally flat, even though I set my little charge on the center of the disc and allowed it to revolve at a dizzy pace, which frolic usually sent it into spasms of excited giggling. Something was wrong. It was under emotional stress of the most racking kind.

I consulted Klunzinger's " Die Korallenthiere des Rothen Meeres " and there found that at an early age the polyp is quite likely to become the victim of a sentimental passion which is directed at its own self.

In other words, my tiny companion was in love with itself, bitterly, desperately, head-over-heels in love.

In an attempt to divert it from this madness, I took it on an extended tour of the Continent, visiting all the old cathedrals and stopping at none but the best hotels. The malady grew worse, instead of better. I thought that perhaps the warm sun of Granada would bring the color back into those pale tentacles, but there the inevitable romance in the soft air was only fuel to the flame, and, in the shadow of the Alhambra, my little polyp gave up the fight and died of a broken heart without ever having declared its love to itself.

I returned to America shortly after not a little chastened by what I had witnessed of Nature's wonders in the realm of passion.

XIX

HOLT! WHO GOES THERE ?

THE reliance of young mothers on Dr. Emmett
Holt's " The Care and Feeding of Children,"
has become a national custom. Especially during
the early infancy of the first baby does the
son rise and set by what " Holt says." But there
are several questions which come to mind which
are not included in the handy questionnaire
arranged by the noted child-specialist, and as he is
probably too busy to answer them himself, we have
compiled an appendix which he may incorporate in
the next edition of his book, if he cares to. Of
course, if he doesn't care to it isn't compulsory.

BATHING

*What should the parent wear while bathing the
child?*

A rubber loin-cloth will usually be sufficient, with
perhaps a pair of elbow-guards and anti-skid gloves.
A bath should never be given a child until at least

[96]

one hour after eating (that is, after the parent has eaten).

What are the objections to face-cloths as a means of bathing children?

They are too easily swallowed, and after six or seven wet face-cloths have been swallowed, the child is likely to become heavy and lethargic.

Under what circumstances should the daily tub-bath be omitted?

Almost any excuse will do. The bath-room may be too cold, or too hot, or the child may be too sleepy or too wide-awake, or the parent may have lame knees or lead poisoning. And anyway, the child had a good bath yesterday.

CLOTHING

How should the infant be held during dressing and undressing?

Any carpenter will be glad to sell you a vise which can be attached to the edge of the table. Place the infant in the vise and turn the screw until there is a slight redness under the pressure. Be careful not to turn it too tight or the child will resent it; but on the other hand, care should be taken not to leave it too loose, otherwise the child will be continually

[97]

falling out on the floor, and you will never get it dressed that way.

What are the most important items in the baby's clothing?

The safety-pins which are in the bureau in the next room.

WEIGHT

How should a child be weighed?

Place the child in the scales. The father should then sit on top of the child to hold him down. Weigh father and child together. Then deduct the father's weight from the gross tonnage, and the weight of the child is the result.

FRESH AIR

What are the objections to an infant's sleeping out-of-doors?

Sleeping out-of-doors in the city is all right, but children sleeping out of doors in the country are likely to be kissed by wandering cows and things. This should never be permitted under any circumstances.

DEVELOPMENT

When does the infant first laugh aloud?

When father tries to pin it up for the first time.

[98]

HOLT! WHO GOES THERE?

*If at two years the child makes no attempt to talk,
what should be suspected?*

That it hasn't yet seen anyone worth talking to.

What should not be fed to a child?

Ripe olives.

*How do we know how much food a healthy child
needs?*

By listening carefully.

*Which parent should go and get the child's early
morning bottle?*

The one least able to feign sleep.

XX

THE COMMITTEE ON THE WHOLE

A NEW plan has just been submitted for running the railroads. That makes one hundred
and eleven.

The present suggestion involves the services of
some sixteen committees. Now presumably the
idea is to get the roses back into the cheeks of the
railroads, so that they will go running about from
place to place again and perhaps make a little
money on pleasant Saturdays and Sundays. But if
these proposed committees are anything like other
committees which we have had to do with, the following will be a fair example of how our railroads
will be run.

The sub-committee on the Punching of Rebate
Slips will have a meeting called for five o'clock in
the private grill-room at the Pan-American Building. Postcards will have been sent out the day before by the Secretary, saying: " Please try to be
present as there are several important matters to be
brought up." This will so pique the curiosity of
the members that they will hardly be able to wait

until five o'clock. One will come at four o'clock by mistake and, after steaming up and down the corridor for half an hour, will go home and send in his resignation.

At 5:10 the Secretary will bustle in with a brief-case and a map showing the weather areas over the entire United States for the preceding year. He will be very warm from hurrying.

At 5:15 two members of the committee will stroll in, one of them saying to the other: " — so the Irishman turns to the Jew and says: 'Well, I knew your father before that!' Aha-ha-ha-ha-ha-ha! 'I knew your father before that!'"

They will then seat themselves at one end of the committee-table, just as another member comes hurrying in. Time 5:21.

One of the story-tellers being the Chairman, he will pound half-heartedly on the table and say: "As some of us have to get away early, I think that we had better begin now, although Mr. Entwhistle and Dr. Pearly are not here."

"I met Dr. Pearly last night at the Vegetarian Club dinner," says one of the members, "and he said that he might be a little late today but that he would surely come."

"His wife has just had a very delicate throat operation, I understand," offers a committeeman who is drawing concentric circles on his pad of paper.

" Bad weather for throat operations," says the Secretary.

" That's right," says the Chairman, looking through a pile of papers for one which he has left at home. " But let's get down to business. At the last meeting the question arose as to whether or not it was advisable to continue having conductors punch the little hole at the bottom of rebate slips. As you know, the slip says, ' Not redeemable if punched here.' Now, someone brought up the point that it seems silly to give out a rebate slip at all if there isn't going to be any rebate on it. A sub-committee was appointed to go into the matter, and I would like to ask Mr. Twing, the chairman, what he has to report."

Mr. Twing will clear his throat and start to speak, but will make only an abortive sound. He will then clear his throat again.

" Mr. Chairman, the other members of the sub-committee and myself were unable to get exactly the data on this that we wanted and I delegated Mr. Entwhistle to dig up something which he said he had read recently in the files of the *Scientific American*. But Mr. Entwhistle doesn't seem to be here today, and so I am unable to report his findings.

"That's right," says the chairman.

It was, however, the sense of the meeting that the conductors should not."

"Should not what?" inquires Dr. Pearly, who has just sneaked in, knocking three hats to the floor while hanging up his coat.

Dr. Pearly is never answered, for the Chairman looks at his watch and says: "I'm very sorry, gentlemen, but I have an appointment at 5:45 and must be going. Supposing I appoint a sub-committee consisting of Dr. Pearly, Mr. Twing and Mr. Berry, to find Mr. Entwhistle and see what he dug out of the files of the *Scientific American.* Then, at the next meeting we can have a report from both sub-committees and will also hear from Professor McKlicktric, who has just returned from Panama. . . . A motion to adjourn is now in order. Do I hear such a motion?"

After listening carefully, he hears it, and the railroads run themselves for another week.

XXI

NOTING AN INCREASE IN BIGAMY

EITHER more men are marrying more wives than ever before, or they are getting more careless about it. During the past week bigamy has crowded baseball out of the papers, and while this may be due in part to the fact that it was a cold, rainy week and little baseball could be played, yet there is a tendency to be noted there somewhere. All those wishing to note a tendency will continue on into the next paragraph.

There is, of course, nothing new in bigamy. Anyone who goes in for it with the idea of originating a new fad which shall be known by his name, like the daguerreotype or potatoes O'Brien, will have to reckon with the priority claims of several hundred generations of historical characters, most of them wearing brown beards. Just why beards and bigamy seem to have gone hand in hand through the ages is a matter for the professional humorists to determine. We certainly haven't got time to do it here.

But the multiple-marriages unearthed during the

past week have a certain homey flavor lacking in
some of those which have gone before. For instance, the man in New Jersey who had two wives
living right with him all of the time in the same
apartment. No need for subterfuge here, no de-
ceiving one about the other. It was just a matter
of walking back and forth between the dining-room
and the study. This is, of course, bigamy under
ideal conditions.

But in tracing a tendency like this, we must not
deal so much with concrete cases as with drifts and
curves. A couple of statistics are also necessary,
especially if it is an alarming tendency that is being
traced. The statistics follow, in alphabetical
order:

In the United States during the years 1918–1919
there were 4,956,673 weddings. 2,485,845 of these
were church weddings, strongly against the wishes
of the bridegrooms concerned. In these weddings
10,489,392 silver olive-forks were received as gifts.

Starting with these figures as a basis, we turn to
the report of the Pennsylvania State Committee on
Outdoor Gymnastics for the year beginning January
4th, 1920, and ending a year later.

This report being pretty fairly uninteresting, we
leave it and turn to another report, which covers
the manufacture and sale of rugs. This has a

picture of a rug in it, and a darned good likeness
it is, too.

In this rug report we find that it takes a Navajo
Indian only eleven days to weave a rug 12 x 5, with
a swastika design in the middle. Eleven days. It
seems incredible. Why, it takes only 365 days to
make a year!

Now, having seen that there are 73,000 men and
women in this country today who can neither read
nor write, and that of these only 4%, or a little over
half, are colored, what are we to conclude? What
is to be the effect on our national morale? Who
is to pay this gigantic bill for naval armament?

Before answering these questions any further
than this, let us quote from an authority on the
subject, a man who has given the best years, or at
any rate some very good years, of his life to research in this field, and who now takes exactly the
stand which we have been outlining in this article.

" I would not," he says in a speech delivered
before the Girls' Friendly Society of Laurel Hill,
" I would not for one minute detract from the glory
of those who have brought this country to its
present state of financial prominence among the
nations of the world, and yet as I think back on
those dark days, I am impelled to voice the protest
of millions of American citizens yet unborn."

LOVE CONQUERS ALL

Perhaps some of our little readers remember what the major premise of this article was. If so, will they please communicate with the writer.

Oh, yes! Bigamy!

Well, it certainly is funny how many cases of bigamy you hear about nowadays. Either more men are marrying more wives than ever before, or they are getting more careless about it. (That sounds very, very familiar. It is barely possible that it is the sentence with which this article opens. We say so many things in the course of one article that repetitions are quite likely to creep in).

At any rate, the tendency seems to be toward an increase in bigamy.

XXII

THE REAL WIGLAF: MAN AND
MONARCH

Much time has been devoted of late by ardent biographers to shedding light on misunderstood characters in history, especially British rulers. We cannot let injustice any longer be done to King Wiglaf, the much-maligned monarch of central Britain in the early Ninth Century.

The fall of the kingdom of Mercia in 828 under the the onslaughts of Ecgberht the West-Saxon, have been laid to Wiglaf's untidy personal habits and his alleged mania for practical joking. The accompanying biographical sketch may serve to disclose some of the more intimate details of the character of the man and to alter in some degree history's unfavorable estimate of him.

OUR first glimpse of the Wiglaf who was one day to become ruler of Mercia, the heart of present-day England (music, please), is when at the age of seven he was taken by Oswier, his father's murderer, to see Mrs. Siddons play *Lady Macbeth*. (Every subject of biographical treatment, regardless of the period in which he or she lived, must have been taken at an early age to see Mrs. Siddons play *Lady Macbeth*. It is part of the code of biography.)

THE REAL WIGLAF

While sitting in the royal box, the young prince Wiglaf was asked what he thought of the performance. "Rotten!" he answered, and left the place abruptly, setting fire to the building as he went out.

Beobald, in citing the above incident in his "Chronicles of Comical Kings," calls it "an hendy hap ichabbe y-hent." And perhaps he's right.

Events proceeded in rapid succession after this for the young boy and we next find him facing marriage with a stiff upper-lip. Mystery has always surrounded the reasons which led to the choice of Princess Offa as Wiglaf's bride. In fact, it has never been quite certain whether or not she *was* his bride. No one ever saw them together.[1] On several occasions he is reported to have asked his chamberlain who she was as she passed by on the street.[2]

And yet the theory persists that she was his wife, owing doubtless to the fact that on the eve of the Battle of Otford he sent a message to her asking where "in God's name" his clean shirts had been put when they came back from the wash.

We come now to that period in Wiglaf's life which has been for so many centuries the cause of his-

[1] Lebody. *Witnesses of the Proximity of Wiglaf to Offa.* II. 265.

[2] Rouguet. *Famous Questions in History.* III. 467.

torical speculation, pro and con. The reference is, of course, to his dealings with Aethelbald, the ambassador from Wessex. Every schoolboy has taken part in the Wiglaf-Aethelbald controversy, but how many really know the inside facts of the case?

Examination of the correspondence between these two men shows Wiglaf to have been simply a great, big-hearted, overgrown boy in the whole affair. All claims of his having had an eye on the throne of Northumbria fade away under the delightful ingenuousness of his attitude as expressed in these letters.

"I should of thought," he writes in 821 to his sister, "that anyone who was not cock-ide drunk would have known better than to of tried to walk bear-foot through that eel-grass from the beech up to the bath-house without sneekers on, which is what that ninn Aethelbald tryed to do this AM. Well say laffter is no name for what you would of done if you had seen him. He looked like he was trying to walk a tide-rope. Hey I yelled at him all the way, do you think you are trying to walk a tide-rope? Well say maybe that didnt make him sore."

Shortly after this letter was written, Wiglaf ascended the throne of Mercia, his father having disappeared Saturday night without trace. A peasant [1] some years after said that he met the old king walking along a road near what is now the Scottish border, telling people that he was carrying a letter of greeting from the Mayor of Pontygn to the Mayor of Langoscgirh. Others say that he fell into the sea off the coast of Wales and became what is now known as King's Rocks. This last has never been authenticated.

At any rate, the son, on ascending the throne, became king. His first official act was to order dinner. " A nice, juicy steak," he is said to have called for,[2] " French fries, apple pie and a cup of coffee." It is probable that he really said " a coff of cuppee," however, as he was a wag of the first water and loved a joke as well as the next king.

We are now thrown into the maelstrom of contradictory historical data, some of which credits Wiglaf with being the greatest ruler Mercia ever had and some of which indicates that he was nothing but a royal bum. It is not the purpose of this biography to try to settle the dispute. All we know for a fact is that he was a very human man who had faults like the rest of us and that shortly after becoming king he disappears from view.

[1] *Peasant Tales and Fun-making.* II. 965.

[2] *Fifty Menus for August.* — 46.

LOVE CONQUERS ALL

His reign began at 4 P. M. one Wednesday (no, Thursday) afternoon and early the next morning Mercia was overrun by the West-Saxons. It is probable that King Wiglaf was sold for old silver to help pay expenses.

XXIII

FACING THE BOYS' CAMP
PROBLEM

THE time seemed to have come to send Junior away to a boys' camp for the summer. He was getting too large to have about the house during the hot weather, and besides, getting him out of town seemed the only way to stop the radio concerts which had been making a continuous Chautauqua of our home-life ever since March.

I therefore got out a magazine and turned to that section of the advertising headed, "Summer Camps and Schools." There was a staggering array. Judging from the photographs the entire child population of the United States spent last summer in bathing suits or on horseback, and the pictures of them were so generic and familiar-looking that there was a great temptation to spend the evening scrutinizing them closely to see if you could pick out anyone you knew.

"Come on, read some out loud," said Doris in her practical way.

" ' The Nooga-Wooga Camps,' " I began. " ' The

Garden Spot of the Micasset Mountains. Tumbling water, calls of birds, light-hearted laughter, horseback rides along shady trails, lasting friendships — all these are the heritage of happy days at Nooga-Wooga.' . . . I don't think much of the costumes they give the boys to wear at Nooga-Wooga. They look rather sissy to me."

" That's because you are looking at the Camps for Girls, dear," said Doris. " Those are girls in Peter Thompsons and bloomers."

Hurriedly turning the page, I came to Camps for Boys.

" ' Camp Wicomagisset, for Manly Boys. On famous Lake Pogoniblick in the heart of the far-famed Wappahammock district. Campfire stories, military drill, mountain climbing, swimming, wading, hiking, log-cabins, sailing —' they say nothing about horseshoeing. Don't you suppose they teach horseshoeing? "

" That probably comes in the second year for the older boys," said Doris. " I wouldn't want Junior to plunge right into horseshoeing his first season. We mustn't rush him."

" ' Camp Wad-ne-go-gallup on the shores of Crisco Bay, Maine. Facing that grandest of all oceans, the Atlantic. Located among the best farms where fresh and wholesome food can be had in abundance ' — yes but *is* it had, my dear? That's the question. Anyway, I don't like the looks of the boat in the picture. It's too full of boys."

" ' Opossum Mountain Camp for Boys. Unusual sports and trips ' — Ah, possibly condor stalking! That certainly would be unusual. But dangerous! I'd hate to think of Junior crawling about over ledges, stalking condors. And it says here that there is a dietitian and a camp-mother, as well."

" Camp-mother? " Doris sniffed, " Probably she thinks she knows how to bring up children — "

Just then Junior came in to announce that he had signed up for a job for the summer, working on the farm of Eddie Westover's uncle. So in view of this added income, I felt that I could afford a little vacation myself, and am leaving on July 1st for Camp Mionogonett in the foothills of the Rokomokos, " a Paradise for Manly Men."

XXIV

ALL ABOUT THE SILESIAN
PROBLEM

SO much controversy has been aroused over
Silesia it is high time that the average man in
this country had a clearer idea of the problem.
At present many people think that if you add oxy-
gen to Silesia you will get oxide of silesia and can
take spots out of clothes with it.

A definite statement of the whole Upper Silesian
question is therefore due, and, for those who care
to listen, about to be made.

The trouble started at the treaty of Noblitz in
1773. You have no idea what a perfectly rotten
treaty that was. It was negotiated by the Grand
Duke Ludwig of Saxe-Goatherd-Cobalt, whose sister married a Morrisey and settled in Fall River.
The aim and ambition of Ludwig's life was to annex
Spielzeugingen to Nichtrauschen, thereby augment-
ing his duchy and at the same time having a dandy
time. And he was the kind of man who would stop
at nothing when it came time to augment his duchy.

In this treaty, then, Ludwig insisted on a clause

making Silesia a monogamy. This was very clever, as it brought the Centrist party in Silesia into direct conflict with the party who wanted to restore the young Prince Niblick to the throne; thereby causing no end of trouble and nasty feeling.

With these obstacles out of the way, the greed and ambition of Ludwig were practically unrestrained. In fact, some historians say that they knew no bounds. Summoning the Storkrath, or common council (composed of three classes: the nobles, the welterweights, and the licensed pilots) he said to them: (according to Taine)

"An army can travel ten days on its stomach, but who the hell wants to be an army?"

This saying has become a by-word in history and is now remembered long after the Grand Duke Ludwig has been forgotten. But at the time, Ludwig received nothing short of an ovation for it, and succeeded in winning over the obstructionists to his side. This made everyone in favor of his disposition of Silesia except the Silesians. And, as they could neither read nor write, they thought that they still belonged to Holland and cheered a dyke every time they saw one.

The question remained in abeyance therefore, for a century and a quarter. Then, in 1895, three years after the accession of Ralph Rittenhouse to the throne of England, the storm broke again. The occasion was the partition of Parchesie by the Great Powers, by which the towns of Zweiback, Ulmhausen and Ost Wilp were united to form what is known as the " industrial triangle " on the Upper Silesian border. These towns are situated in the heart of the pumice district and could alone supply France and Germany with pumice for fifty years, provided it didn't rain. Bismarck once called Ost Wilp " the pumice heart of the world," and he was about right, too.

It will therefore be seen how important it was to France that this " industrial triangle " on the Silesian border should belong to Germany. At the conference which designated the border line, Gambetta, representing France, insisted that the line should follow the course of the Iser River (" iser on one side or the other," was the way he is reported to have phrased it), which would divide the pumice deposits into three areas, the fourth being the dummy. This would never do.

Experts were called in to see if it might not be possible to so divide the district that France might get a quarter, Germany a quarter and England fifty cents. It was suggested that the line be drawn down through Globe-Wernicke to the mouth of the Iser. As Gambetta said, the line had to be drawn somewhere and it might as well be there. But Lord Hay-Paunceforte, representing England, refused to concede the point and for a time it looked like an open breach. But matters were smoothed over by the holding of a plebiscite in all the towns of Upper Silesia. The result of this plebiscite was taken and exactly reversed by the council, so that the entire Engadine Valley was given to Sweden, who didn't want it anyway.

And there the matter now stands.

XXV

"HAPPY THE HOME WHERE BOOKS ARE FOUND"

BY way of egging people on to buy Dr. Eliot's Five Foot Shelf of books, the publishers are resorting to an advertisement in which are depicted two married couples, one reading together by the library table, the other playing some two-handed game of cards which is evidently boring them considerably. The query is "Which One of These Couples Will be the Happier in Five Years?" the implication being that the young people who buy Dr. Eliot's books will, by constant reading aloud to each other from the works of the world's best writers, cement a companionship which will put to shame the illiterate union of the young card players.

Granted that most two-handed games of cards *are* dull enough to result in divorce at the end of five years, they cannot be compared to co-operative family reading as a system of home-wrecking. If this were a betting periodical, we would have ten dollars to place on the chance of the following being the condition of affairs in the literary family at the end of the stated time:

(*The husband is reading his evening newspaper. The wife appears, bringing a volume from the Five Foot Shelf. Tonight it is Darwin's " Origin of Species."*)

WIFE: Hurry up and finish that paper. We'll never get along in this Darwin if we don't begin earlier than we did last night.

HUSBAND: Well, suppose we didn't get along in it. That would suit me all right.

WIFE: If you don't want me to read it to you, just say so . . . (*after-thought*) if it's so far over your head, just say so.

HUSBAND: It's not over my head at all. It's just dull. Why don't you read some more out of that Italian novel?

WIFE: Ugh! I hate that. I suppose you'd rather have me read " The Sheik."

HUSBAND (*nastily*): No-I-wouldn't-rather-have-you-read- " The Sheik." Go on ahead with your Darwin. I'm listening.

WIFE: It's not *my* Darwin. I simply want to know a little something, that's all. Of course, *you* know everything, so you don't have to read anything more.

LOVE CONQUERS ALL

HUSBAND: Go on, go on.

WIFE: That last book we read was so far over —

HUSBAND: Go on, go on.

WIFE: (*reads in an injured tone one and a half pages on the selective processes of pigeons*): You're asleep!

HUSBAND: I am not. The last words you read were " to this conclusion."

WIFE: Yes, well, what were the words before that?

HUSBAND: How should I know? I'm not learning the thing to recite somewhere, am I?

WIFE: Well, it's very funny that you didn't notice when I read the last sentence backwards. And if you weren't asleep what were you doing with your eyes closed?

HUSBAND: I got smoke in them and was resting them for a minute. Haven't I got a right to rest my eyes a minute?

WIFE: I suppose it rests your eyes to breathe through your mouth and hold your head way over on one side.

HUSBAND: Yes it does, and wha'd'yer think of *that?*

"If you weren't asleep what were you doing with your eyes closed?"

WHERE BOOKS ARE FOUND

WIFE: Go on and read your newspaper. That's just about your mental speed.

HUSBAND: I'm perfectly willing to read books in this set if you'd pick any decent ones.

WIFE: Yes, you are.

HUSBAND: Wha'd'yer mean " Yes you are "?

WIFE: Just what I said.

(*This goes on for ten minutes and then husband draws a revolver and kills his wife.*)

XXVI

WHEN NOT IN ROME, WHY DO AS THE ROMANS DID?

THERE is a growing sentiment among sign painters that when a sign or notice is to be put up in a public place it should be written in characters that are at least legible, so that, to quote " The Manchester Guardian " (as every one seems to do) " He who runs may read."

This does not strike one as being an unseemly pandering to popular favor. The supposition is that the sign is put there to be read, otherwise it would have been turned over to an inmate of the Odd Fellows Home to be engraved on the head of a pin. And what could be a more fair requirement than that it should be readable?

Advertising, with its billboard message of rustless screens and co-educational turkish-baths, has done much to further the good cause, and a glance through the files of newspapers of seventy-five years ago, when the big news story of the day was played up in diamond type easily deciphered in a strong light with the naked eye, shows that news printing has not, to use a slang phrase, stood still.

But in the midst of this uniform progress we find a stagnant spot. Surrounded by legends that are patent and easy to read and understand, we find the stone-cutter and the architect still putting up tablets and cornerstones, monuments and cornices, with dates disguised in Roman numerals. It is as if it were a game, in which they were saying, " The number we are thinking of is even; it begins with M; it has five digits and when they are spread out, end to end, they occupy three feet of space. You have until we count to one hundred to guess what it is."

Roman numerals are all right for a rainy Sunday afternoon or to take a convalescent's mind from his illness, but to put them in a public place, where the reader stands a good chance of being run over by a dray if he spends more than fifty seconds in their perusal, is not in keeping with the efficiency of the age. If for no other reason than the extra space they take, involving more marble, more of the cutter's time and wear and tear on his instruments, not to mention the big overhead, you would think that Roman numerals would have been abolished long ago.

Of course, they can be figured out if you're good

at that sort of thing. By working on your cuff and backs of envelopes, you can translate them in no time at all compared to the time taken by a cocoon to change into a butterfly, for instance. All you have to do is remember that " M " stands for either " *millium*," meaning thousand, or for " million." By referring to the context you can tell which is more probable. If, for example, it is a date, you can tell right away that it doesn't mean " million," for there isn't any " million " in our dates. And there is one-seventh or eighth of your number deciphered already. Then " C," of course, stands for " *centum*," which you can translate by working backwards at it, taking such a word as " century " or " per cent," and looking up what they come from, and there you have it! By this time it is hardly the middle of the afternoon, and all you have before you is a combination of X's, I's and an L, the latter standing for " Elevated Railway," and " Licorice," or, if you cross it with two little horizontal lines, it stands for the English pound, which is equivalent to about four dollars and eighty-odd cents in real money. Simple as sawing through a log.

But it takes time. That's the big trouble with it. You can't do the right thing by the office and go in for Roman numerals, too. And since most of the people who pass such inscriptions are dependent on their own earnings, why not cater to them a bit and let them in on the secret?

Probably the only reason that the people haven't risen up and demanded a reform along these lines is because so few of them really give a hang what the inscription says. If the American Antiquarian Turn-Verein doesn't care about stating in understandable figures the date on which the cornerstone of their building was laid, the average citizen is perfectly willing to let the matter drop right there.

But it would never do to revert to Roman numerals in, say, the arrangement of time-tables. How long would the commuter stand it if he had to mumble to himself for twenty minutes and use up the margins of his newspaper before he could figure out what was the next train after the 5:18? Or this, over the telephone between wife and husband:

" Hello, dear! I think I'll come in town for lunch. What trains can I get? "

" Just a minute — I'll look them up. Hold the wire. . . . Let's see, here's one at XII:LVIII, that's twelve, and L is a thousand and V is five and three I's are three; that makes 12:one thousand. . . . that can't be right. . . . now XII certainly is twelve, and L . . . what does L stand for? . . . I say, what — does — L — stand — for? . . . Well,

ask Helma. . . . What does she say? . . . Fifty?
. . . Sure, that makes it come out all right. . . .
12:58. . . . What time is it now? . . . 1 o'clock?
. . . Well, the next one leaves Oakam at I:XLIV.
. . . that's . . . " etc.

Batting averages and the standing of teams in
the leagues are another department where the introduction of Roman numerals would be suicide for
the political party in power at the time. For of all
things that are essential to the day's work of the
voter, an early enlightenment in the matter of the
home team's standing and the numerical progress
of the favorite batsman are of primary importance.
This information has to be gleaned on the way to
work in the morning, and, except for those who
come in to work each day from North Philadelphia
or the Croton Reservoir, it would be a physical
impossibility to figure the tables out and get any
of the day's news besides.

CLVB BATTING RECORDS

	Games	At Bat	Runs	B.H.	S.B.	S.H.	Aver.
Detroit	CLII	MMMMMXXCIX	DCLIII	MCCCXXXIII	CLXVIII	CC	CCLXII
Chicago	CLI	MMMMCMXL	DLXXI	MCCXLVI	CLXXIX	CCXXI	CCLII
Cleveland	CLII	MMMMCMXXXVII	DCXIX	MCCXXXI	CL	CCXXI	CCXLIX
Boston	CLI	MMMMDCCCLXXIV	DXXXIV	MCXCI	CXXXVI	CCXXXV	CCXLV
New York	CL	MMMMCMLXXXVII	DLIV	MCCXXX	CLXXV	CLXV	CCXLVII
Washington	CLIII	MMMMCMXXVIII	DV	MCXC	CLXIII	CLXV	CCXDI
St. Louis	CLV	MMMMMLXV	DLXXIV	MCCXXI	CCVII	CLXII	CCXLI
Philadelphia	CXLIX	MMMMDCCCXXVI	CCCCXVI	MCXLIII	CXLIII	CLV	CCXXXVII

YOU CAN'T DO RIGHT BY THE OFFICE AND GO IN FOR
ROMAN NUMERALS TOO.

WHY DO AS THE ROMANS DID?

On matters such as these the proletariat would have protested the Roman numeral long ago. If they are willing to let its reactionary use on tablets and monuments stand it is because of their indifference to influences which do not directly affect their pocketbooks. But if it could be put up to them in a powerful cartoon, showing the Architect and the Stone-Cutter dressed in frock coats and silk hats, with their pockets full of money, stepping on the Common People so that he cannot see what is written on the tablet behind them, then perhaps the public would realize how they are being imposed on.

For that there is an organized movement among architects and stone-cutters to keep these things from the citizenry there can no longer be any doubt. It is not only a matter of the Roman numerals. How about the use of the " V " when " U " should be used? You will always see it in inscriptions. " SVMNER BVILDING " is one of the least offensive. Perhaps the excuse is that " V " is more adapted to stone-lettering. Then why not carry this principle out further? Why not use the letter H when S is meant? Or substitute K for B? If the idea is to deceive, and to make it easier for the stone-cutter, a pleasing effect could be got from the inscription, " Erected in 1897 by the Society

of Arts and Grafts", by making it read: " EKEA-
TEW IZ MXIXLXIXLXXII LY THE XNLIEZY
OF AEXA ZNL ELAFTX." There you have
letters that are all adapted to stone-cutting; they
look well together, and they are, in toto, as intel-
ligible as most inscriptions.

XXVII

THE TOOTH, THE WHOLE TOOTH, AND
NOTHING BUT THE TOOTH

SOME well-known saying (it doesn't make much difference what) is proved by the fact that everyone likes to talk about his experiences at the dentist's. For years and years little articles like this have been written on the subject, little jokes like some that I shall presently make have been made, and people in general have been telling other people just what emotions they experience when they crawl into the old red plush guillotine.

They like to explain to each other how they feel when the dentist puts " that buzzer thing " against their bicuspids, and, if sufficiently pressed, they will describe their sensations on mouthing a rubber dam.

" I'll tell you what I hate," they will say with great relish, " when he takes that little nut-pick and begins to scrape. Ugh! "

" Oh, I'll tell you what's worse than that," says the friend, not to be outdone, " when he is poking around careless-like, and strikes a nerve. Wow! "

And if there are more than two people at the

LOVE CONQUERS ALL

experience-meeting, everyone will chip in and tell
what he or she considers to be the worst phase of
the dentist's work, all present enjoying the narra-
tion hugely and none so much as the narrator who
has suffered so.

This sort of thing has been going on ever since
the first mammoth gold tooth was hung out as a
bait to folks in search of a good time. (By the
way, when *did* the present obnoxious system of den-
tistry begin? It can't be so very long ago that the
electric auger was invented, and where would a
dentist be without an electric auger? Yet you
never hear of Amalgam Filling Day, or any other
anniversary in the dental year). There must be
a conspiracy of silence on the part of the trade to
keep hidden the names of the men who are responsible for all this).

However many years it may be that dentists have
been plying their trade, in all that time people have
never tired of talking about their teeth. This is
probably due to the inscrutable workings of Nature
who is always supplying new teeth to talk about.

As a matter of fact, the actual time and suffering
in the chair is only a fraction of the gross expendi-
ture connected with the affair. The preliminary
period, about which nobody talks, is much the
worse. This dates from the discovery of the way-

ward tooth and extends to the moment when the dentist places his foot on the automatic hoist which jacks you up into range. Giving gas for tooth-extraction is all very humane in its way, but the time for anaesthetics is when the patient first decides that he must go to the dentist. From then on, until the first excavation is started, should be shrouded in oblivion.

There is probably no moment more appalling than that in which the tongue, running idly over the teeth in a moment of care-free play, comes suddenly upon the ragged edge of a space from which the old familiar filling has disappeared. The world stops and you look meditatively up to the corner of the ceiling. Then quickly you draw your tongue away, and try to laugh the affair off, saying to yourself:

" Stuff and nonsense, my good fellow! There is nothing the matter with your tooth. Your nerves are upset after a hard day's work, that's all."

Having decided this to your satisfaction, you slyly, and with a poor attempt at being casual, slide the tongue back along the line of adjacent teeth, hoping against hope that it will reach the end without mishap.

But there it is! There can be no doubt about it this time. The tooth simply has got to be filled

by someone, and the only person who can fill it
with anything permanent is a dentist. You wonder
if you might not be able to patch it up yourself for
the time being, — a year or so — perhaps with a
little spruce-gum and a coating of new-skin. It is
fairly far back, and wouldn't have to be a very
sightly job.

But this has an impracticable sound, even to you.
You might want to eat some peanut-brittle (you
never can tell when someone might offer you
peanut-brittle these days), and the new-skin, while
serviceable enough in the case of cream soups and
custards, couldn't be expected to stand up under
heavy crunching.

So you admit that, since the thing has got to
be filled, it might as well be a dentist who does the
job.

This much decided, all that is necessary is to
call him up and make an appointment.

Let us say that this resolve is made on Tuesday.
That afternoon you start to look up the dentist's
number in the telephone-book. A great wave of
relief sweeps over you when you discover that it
isn't there. How can you be expected to make an
appointment with a man who hasn't got a telephone? And how can you have a tooth filled without making an appointment? The whole thing is

impossible, and that's all there is to it. God knows you did your best.

On Wednesday there is a slightly more insistent twinge, owing to bad management of a sip of ice-water. You decide that you simply must get in touch with that dentist when you get back from lunch. But you know how those things are. First one thing and then another came up, and a man came in from Providence who had to be shown around the office, and by the time you had a minute to yourself it was five o'clock. And, anyway, the tooth didn't bother you again. You wouldn't be surprised if, by being careful, you could get along with it as it is until the end of the week when you will have more time. A man has to think of his business, after all, and what is a little personal discomfort in the shape of an unfilled tooth to the satisfaction of work well done in the office?

By Saturday morning you are fairly reconciled to going ahead, but it is only a half day and probably he has no appointments left, anyway. Monday is really the time. You can begin the week afresh. After all, Monday is really the logical day to start in going to the dentist.

Bright and early Monday morning you make another try at the telephone-book, and find, to your horror, that some time between now and last Tues-

day the dentist's name and number have been
inserted into the directory. There it is. There is
no getting around it: " Burgess, Jas. Kendal, DDS.
. . . Courtland — 2654 ". There is really nothing
left to do but to call him up. Fortunately the line
is busy, which gives you a perfectly good excuse
for putting it over until Tuesday. But on Tuesday luck is against you and you get a clear connection with the doctor himself. An appointment
is arranged for Thursday afternoon at 3:30.

Thursday afternoon, and here it is only Tuesday
morning! Almost anything may happen between
now and then. We might declare war on Mexico,
and off you'd have to go, dentist appointment or no
dentist appointment. Surely a man couldn't let
a date to have a tooth filled stand in the way of his
doing his duty to his country. Or the social revo-
lution might start on Wednesday, and by Thursday
the whole town might be in ashes. You can picture
yourself standing, Thursday afternoon at 3.30 on
the ruins of the City Hall, fighting off marauding
bands of reds, and saying to yourself, with a sigh
of relief: " Only to think! At this time I was to
have been climbing into the dentist's chair! " You
never can tell when your luck will turn in a thing
like that.

But Wednesday goes by and nothing happens.

THE TOOTH AND THE WHOLE TOOTH

And Thursday morning dawns without even a word
from the dentist saying that he has been called
suddenly out of town to lecture before the Incisor
Club. Apparently, everything is working against
you.

By this time, your tongue has taken up a permanent resting-place in the vacant tooth, and is
causing you to talk indistinctly and incoherently.
Somehow you feel that if the dentist opens your
mouth and finds the tip of your tongue in the tooth,
he will be deceived and go away without doing
anything.

The only thing left is for you to call him up and
say that you have just killed a man and are being
arrested and can't possibly keep your appointment.
But any dentist would see through that. He would
laugh right into his transmitter at you. There is
probably no excuse which it would be possible to
invent which a dentist has not already heard eighty
or ninety times. No, you might as well see the
thing through now.

Luncheon is a ghastly rite. The whole left side
of your jaw has suddenly developed an acute sensi-
tiveness and the disaffection has spread to the four
teeth on either side of the original one. You doubt
if it will be possible for him to touch it at all.
Perhaps all he intends to do this time is to look at

it anyway. You might even suggest that to him. You could very easily come in again soon and have him do the actual work.

Three-thirty draws near. A horrible time of day at best. Just when a man's vitality is lowest. Before stepping in out of the sunlight into the building in which the dental parlor is, you take one look about you at the happy people scurrying by in the street. Carefree children that they are! What do they know of Life? Probably that man in the silly-looking hat never had trouble with so much as his baby-teeth. There they go, pushing and jostling each other, just as if within ten feet of them there was not a man who stands on the brink of the Great Misadventure. Ah well! Life is like that!

Into the elevator. The last hope is gone. The door clangs and you look hopelessly about you at the stupid faces of your fellow passengers. How can people be so clownish? Of course, there is always the chance that the elevator will fall and that you will all be terribly hurt. But that is too much to expect. You dismiss it from your thoughts as too impractical, too visionary. Things don't work out as happily as that in real life.

You feel a certain glow of heroic pride when you tell the operator the right floor number. You might

just as easily have told him a floor too high or too
low, and that would, at least, have caused delay.
But after all, a man must prove himself a man and
the least you can do is to meet Fate with an unflinch-
ing eye and give the right floor number.

Too often has the scene in the dentist's waiting-
room been described for me to try to do it again
here. They are all alike. The antiseptic smell,
the ominous hum from the operating-rooms, the 1921
" Literary Digests," and the silent, sullen, group
of waiting patients, each trying to look unconcerned
and cordially disliking everyone else in the room,
— all these have been sung by poets of far greater
lyric powers than mine. (Not that I really think
that they *are* greater than mine, but that's the cus-
tomary form of excuse for not writing something
you haven't got time or space to do. As a matter
of fact, I think I could do it much better than it
has ever been done before).

I can only say that, as you sit looking, with
unseeing eyes, through a large book entitled, " The
Great War in Pictures," you would gladly change
places with the most lowly of God's creatures. It
is inconceivable that there should be anyone worse
off than you, unless perhaps it is some of the poor
wretches who are waiting with you.

That one over in the arm-chair, nervously tearing

to shreds a copy of " The Dental Review and Practical Inlay Worker." She may have something frightful the trouble with her. She couldn't possibly look more worried. Perhaps it is very, very painful. This thought cheers you up considerably. What cowards women are in times like these!

And then there comes the sound of voices from the next room.

" All right, Doctor, and if it gives me any more pain shall I call you up? . . . . Do you think that it will bleed much more? . . . . Saturday morning, then, at eleven. . . . Good bye, Doctor."

And a middle-aged woman emerges (all women are middle-aged when emerging from the dentist's office) looking as if she were playing the big emotional scene in " John Ferguson." A wisp of hair waves dissolutely across her forehead between her eyes. Her face is pale, except for a slight inflammation at the corners of her mouth, and in her eyes is that far-away look of one who has been face to face with Life. But she is through. She should care how she looks.

The nurse appears, and looks inquiringly at each one in the room. Each one in the room evades the nurse's glance in one last, futile attempt to fool someone and get away without seeing the dentist. But she spots you and nods pleasantly. God, how

You would gladly change places with the most lawless of
God's creatures.

pleasantly she nods! There ought to be a law against people being as pleasant as that.

" The doctor will see you now," she says.

The English language may hold a more disagreeable combination of words than " The doctor will see you now." I am willing to concede something to the phrase " Have you anything to say before the current is turned on." That may be worse for the moment, but it doesn't last so long. For continued, unmitigating depression, I know nothing to equal " The doctor will see you now." But I'm not narrow-minded about it. I'm willing to consider other possibilities.

Smiling feebly, you trip over the extended feet of the man next to you, and stagger into the delivery-room, where, amid a ghastly array of death-masks of teeth, blue flames waving eerily from Bunsen burners, and the drowning sound of perpetually running water which chokes and gurgles at intervals, you sink into the chair and close your eyes.

.   .   .   .   .   .

But now let us consider the spiritual exaltation that comes when you are at last let down and turned loose. It is all over, and what did it amount to? Why, nothing at all. A–ha–ha–ha–ha–ha! Nothing at all.

LOVE CONQUERS ALL

You suddenly develop a particular friendship for the dentist. A splendid fellow, really. You ask him questions about his instruments. What does he use this thing for, for instance? Well, well, to think of a little thing like that making all that trouble. A-ha-ha-ha-ha-ha! . . . And the dentist's family, how are they? Isn't that fine!

Gaily you shake hands with him and straighten your tie. Forgotten is the fact that you have another appointment with him for Monday. There is no such thing as Monday. You are through for today, and all's right with the world.

As you pass out through the waiting-room, you leer at the others unpleasantly. The poor fishes! Why can't they take their medicine like grown people and not sit there moping as if they were going to be shot?

Heigh-ho! Here's the elevator-man! A charming fellow! You wonder if he knows that you have just had a tooth filled. You feel tempted to tell him and slap him on the back. You feel tempted to tell everyone out in the bright, cheery street. And what a wonderful street it is too! All full of nice, black snow and water. After all, Life is sweet!

And then you go and find the first person whom you can accost without being arrested and explain to him just what it was that the dentist did to you, and how you felt, and what you have got to have done next time.

Which brings us right back to where we were in the beginning, and perhaps accounts for everyone's liking to divulge their dental secrets to others. It may be a sort of hysterical relief that, for the time being, it is all over with.

XXVIII

MALIGNANT MIRRORS

AS a rule, I try not to look into mirrors any more than is absolutely necessary. Things are depressing enough as they are without my going out of my way to make myself miserable.

But every once in a while it is unavoidable. There are certain mirrors in town with which I am brought face to face on occasion and there is nothing to do but make the best of it. I have come to classify them according to the harshness with which they fling the truth into my face.

I am unquestionably at my worst in the mirror before which I try on hats. I may have been going along all winter thinking of other things, dwelling on what people tell me is really a splendid spiritual side to my nature, thinking of myself as rather a fine sort of person, not dashing perhaps, but one from whose countenance shines a great light of honesty and courage which is even more to be desired than physical beauty. I rather imagine that little children on the street and grizzled Supreme

Court justices out for a walk turn as I pass and say " A fine face. Plain, but fine."

Then I go in to buy a hat. The mirror in the hat store is triplicate, so that you see yourself not only head-on but from each side. The appearance that I present to myself in this mirror is that of three police-department photographs showing all possible approaches to the face of Harry DuChamps, alias Harry Duval, alias Harry Duffy, wanted in Rochester for the murder of Nettie Lubitch, age 5. All that is missing is the longitudinal scar across the right cheek.

I have never seen a meaner face than mine is in the hat-store mirror. I could stand its not being handsome. I could even stand looking weak in an attractive, man-about-town sort of way. But in the right hand mirror there confronts me a hang-dog face, the face of a yellow craven, while at the left leers an even more repulsive type, sensual and cruel.

Furthermore, even though I have had a hair-cut that very day, there is an unkempt fringe showing over my collar in back and the collar itself, (a Wimpet, $14\frac{1}{2}$, which looked so well on the young man in the car-card) seems to be something that would be worn by a Maine guide when he goes into Portland for the day. My suit needs pressing and there is a general air of its having been given to me, with ten dollars, by the State on my departure from Sing Sing the day before.

But for an unfavorable full-length view, nothing can compare with the one that I get of myself as I pass the shoe-store on the corner. They have a mirror in the window, so set that it catches the reflection of people as they step up on the curb. When there are other forms in the picture it is not always easy to identify yourself at first, especially at a distance, and every morning on my way to work, unless I deliberately avert my face, I am mortified to discover that the unpleasant-looking man, with the rather effeminate, swinging gait, whom I see mincing along through the crowd, is none other than myself.

The only good mirror in the list is the one in the elevator of my clothing-store. There is a subdued light in the car, a sort of golden glow which softens and idealizes, and the mirror shows only a two-thirds length, making it impossible to see how badly the cuffs on my trousers bag over the tops of my shoes. Here I become myself again. I have even thought that I might be handsome if I paid as much attention to my looks as some men do. In this mirror, my clothes look (for the last time) as similar clothes look on well-dressed men. A hat which is in every

I am mortified to discover that the unpleasant looking man
is none other than myself.

respect perfect when seen here, immediately becomes a senatorial sombrero when I step out into
the street, but for the brief space of time while I am
in that elevator, I am the *distingué*, clean-cut,
splendid figure of a man that the original blue-prints
called for. I wonder if it takes much experience
to run an elevator, for if it doesn't, I would like to
make my life-work running that car with the magic
mirror.

XXIX

THE POWER OF THE PRESS

THE Police Commissioner of New York City
explains the wave of crime in that city by
blaming the newspapers. The newspapers, he says,
are constantly printing accounts of robberies and
murders, and these accounts simply encourage other
criminals to come to New York and do the same.
If the papers would stop giving all this publicity to
crime, the crooks might forget that there was such
a thing. As it is, they read about it in their newspapers every morning, and sooner or later have to
go out and try it for themselves.

This is a terrible thought, but suggests a convenient alibi for other errant citizens. Thus we
may read the following NEWS NOTES:

Benjamin W. Gleam, age forty-two, of 1946
Ruby Avenue, The Bronx, was arrested last night
for appearing in the Late Byzantine Room of the
Museum of Fine Arts clad only in a suit of medium-
weight underwear. When questioned Gleam said
that he had seen so many pictures in the newspaper
advertisements of respectable men and women going

about in their underwear, drinking tea, jumping hurdles and holding family reunions, that he simply couldn't stand it any longer, and had to try it for himself. "The newspapers did it," he is quoted as saying.

Mrs. Leonia M. Eggcup, who was arrested yesterday on the charge of bigamy, issued a statement today through her attorneys, Wine, Women and Song.

"I am charged with having eleven husbands, all living in various parts of the United States," reads the statement. "This charge is correct. But before I pay the extreme penalty, I want to have the public understand that I am not to blame. It is the fault of the press of this country. Day after day I read the list of marriages in my morning paper. Day after day I saw people after people getting married. Finally the thing got into my blood, and although I was married at the time, I felt that I simply had to be married again. Then, no sooner would I become settled in my new home, than the constant incitement to further matrimonial ventures would come through the columns of the daily press. I fell, it is true, but if there is any justice in this land, it will be the newspapers and not I who will suffer."

XXX

HOME FOR THE HOLIDAYS

A S a pretty tribute to that element of our population which is under twenty-two years of age,
these are called " the Holidays."

This is the only chance that the janitors of the
schools and colleges have to soak the floors of the
recitation halls with oil to catch the dust of the next
semester, and while this is being done there is nothing to do with the students but to send them home
for a week or two. Thus it happened that the
term " holidays " is applied to that period of the
year when everybody else is working just twice as
hard and twice as long during the week to make up
for that precious day which must be lost to the Sales
Campaign or the Record Output on Christmas Day.

For those who are home from school and college
it is called, in the catalogues of their institutions,
a " recess " or " vacation," and the general impression is allowed to get abroad among the parents
that it is to be a period of rest and recuperation.
Arthur and Alice have been working so hard at
school or college that two weeks of good quiet home-

life and home cooking will put them right on their feet again, ready to pitch into that chemistry course in which, owing to an incompetent instructor, they did not do very well last term.

That the theory of rest during vacation is fallacious can be proved by hiding in the coat closet of the home of any college or school youth home for Christmas recess. Admission to the coat closet may be forced by making yourself out to be a government official or an inspector of gas meters. Once hidden among the overshoes, you will overhear the following little earnest drama, entitled " Home for the Holidays."

There was a banging of the front door, and Edgar has arrived. A round of kisses, an exchange of health reports, and Edgar is bounding upstairs.

" Dinner in half an hour," says Mother.

" Sorry," shouts Edgar from the bath-tub, " but I've got to go out to the Whortleberry's to a dinner dance. Got the bid last week. Say, have I got any dress-studs at home here? Mine are in my trunk."

Father's studs are requisitioned and the family cluster at Edgar's door to slide in a few conversational phrases while he is getting the best of his dress shirt.

" How have you been? " (Three guesses as to who it is that asks this.)

" Oh, all right. Say, have I got any pumps at home? Mine are in the trunk. Where are those old ones I had last summer? "

" Don't you want me to tie your tie for you? " (Two guesses as to who it is that asks this.)

" No, thanks. Can I get my laundry done by tomorrow night? I've got to go out to the Clamps' at Short Neck for over the week-end to a bob-sledding party, and when I get back from there Mrs. Dibble is giving a dinner and theatre party."

" Don't you want to eat a little dinner here before you go to the Whortleberry's? " (One guess as to who it is that asks this.)

But Edgar has bounded down the stairs and left the Family to comfort each other with such observations as " He looks tired," " I think that he has filled out a little," or " I wonder if he's studying too hard."

You might stay in the coat-closet for the entire two weeks and not hear much more of Edgar than this. His parents don't. They catch him as he is going up and down stairs and while he is putting the studs into his shirt, and are thankful for that. They really get into closer touch with him while he is at college, for he writes them a weekly letter then.

Nerve-racking as this sort of life is to the youth

who is supposed to be resting during his vacation, it might be even more wearing if he were to stay within the Family precincts. Once in a while one of the parties for which he has been signed up falls through, and he is forced to spend the evening at home. At first it is somewhat embarrassing to be thrown in with strangers for a meal like that, but, as the evening wears on, the ice is broken and things assume a more easy swing. The Family begins to make remarks.

" You must stand up straighter, my boy," says Father, placing his hand between Edgar's shoulder-blades. " You are slouching badly. I noticed it as you walked down the street this morning."

" Do all the boys wear soft-collared shirts like that? " asks Mother. " Personally, I think that they look very untidy. They are all right for tennis and things like that, but I wish you'd put on a starched collar when you are in the house. You never see Elmer Quiggly wearing a collar like that. He always looks neat."

" For heaven's sake, Eddie," says Sister, " take off that tie. You certainly do get the most terrific-looking things to put around your neck. It looks like a Masonic apron. Let me go with you when you buy your next batch."

By this time Edgar has his back against the wall

and is breathing hard. What do these folks know
of what is being done?

If it is not family heckling it may be that even
more insidious trial, the third degree. This is usually inflicted by semi-relatives and neighbors. The
formulæ are something like this:

" Well, how do you like your school? "

" I suppose you have plenty of time for pranks,
eh? "

" What a good time you boys must have! It isn't
so much what you get out of books that will help
you in after life, I have found, but the friendships
made in college. Meeting so many boys from all
parts of the country — why, it's a liberal education
in itself."

" What was the matter with the football team
this season? "

" Let's see, how many more years have you?
What, only one more! Well, well, and I can remember you when you were that high, and used to
come over to my house wearing a little green dress,
with big mother-of-pearl buttons. You certainly
were a cute little boy, and used to call our cook
' Sna-sna.' And here you are, almost a senior."

" Oh, are you 1924? I wonder if you know a
fellow named — er — Mellish — Spencer Mellish?
I met him at the beach last summer. I am pretty

"I can remember you when you were that high."

sure that he is in your class — well, no, maybe it
was 1918."

After an hour or two of this Edgar is willing to
go back to college and take an extra course in Black-
smithing, Chipping and Filing, given during the
Christmas vacation, rather than run the risk of getting caught again. And, whichever way you look
at it, whether he spends his time getting into and
out of his evening clothes, or goes crazy answering
questions and defending his mode of dress, it all
adds up to the same in the end — fatigue and de-
pletion and what the doctor would call " a general
run-down nervous condition."

The younger you are the more frayed you get.
Little Wilbur comes home from school, where he
has been put to bed at 8:30 every night with the
rest of the fifth form boys, and has had to brush
his hair in the presence of the head-master's wife,
and dives into what might be called a veritable
maelstrom of activity. From a diet of cereal and
fruit-whips, he is turned loose in the butler's pantry
among the maraschino cherries and given a free rein
at the various children's parties, where individual
pound-cake Santas and brandied walnuts are followed by an afternoon at " Treasure Island," with
the result that he comes home and insists on tipping

every one in the family the black spot and breaks the cheval glass when he is denied going to the six-day bicycle race at two in the morning.

Little girls do practically the same, and, if they are over fourteen, go back to school with the added burden of an *affaire de cœur* contracted during the recess. In general, it takes about a month or two of good, hard schooling and overstudy to put the child back on its feet after the Christmas rest at home.

Which leads us to the conclusion that our educational system is all wrong. It is obvious that the child should be kept at home for eight months out of the year and sent to school for the vacations.

XXXI

HOW TO UNDERSTAND
INTERNATIONAL FINANCE

IT is high time that someone came out with a clear statement of the international financial situation. For weeks and weeks officials have been rushing about holding conferences and councils and having their pictures taken going up and down the steps of buildings. Then, after each conference, the newspapers have printed a lot of figures showing the latest returns on how much Germany owes the bank. And none of it means anything.

Now there is a certain principle which has to be followed in all financial discussions involving sums over one hundred dollars. There is probably not more than one hundred dollars in actual cash in circulation today. That is, if you were to call in all the bills and silver and gold in the country at noon tomorrow and pile them up on the table, you would find that you had just about one hundred dollars, with perhaps several Canadian pennies and a few peppermint life-savers. All the rest of the money you hear about doesn't exist. It is conversation-money. When you hear of a transaction involving $50,000,000 it means that one firm wrote " 50,000,000 " on a piece of paper and gave it to another firm, and the other firm took it home and said " Look, Momma, I got $50,000,000! " But when Momma asked for a dollar and a quarter out of it to pay the man who washed the windows, the answer probably was that the firm hadn't got more than seventy cents in cash.

This is the principle of finance. So long as you can pronounce any number above a thousand, you have got that much money. You can't work this scheme with the shoe-store man or the restaurant-owner, but it goes big on Wall St. or in international financial circles.

This much understood, we see that when the Allies demand 132,000,000,000 gold marks from Germany they know very well that nobody in Germany has ever seen 132,000,000,000 gold marks and never will. A more surprised and disappointed lot of boys you couldn't ask to see than the Supreme Financial Council would be if Germany were actually to send them a money-order for the full amount demanded.

What they mean is that, taken all in all, Germany owes the world 132,000,000,000 gold marks plus carfare. This includes everything, breakage, meals sent to room, good will, everything. Now, it is understood that if they really meant this, Germany couldn't even draw cards; so the principle on which the thing is figured out is as follows: (Watch this closely; there is a trick in it).

You put down a lot of figures, like this. Any figures will do, so long as you can't read them quickly:

132,000,000,000 gold marks

$33,000,000,000 on a current value basis

$21,000,000,000 on reparation account plus $12\frac{1}{2}\%$ yearly tax on German exports

11,000,000,000 gold fish

$1.35 amusement tax

866,000 miles. Diameter of the sun

2,000,000,000

27,000,000,000

31,000,000,000

Then you add them together and subtract the number you first thought of. This leaves 11. And the card you hold in your hand is the seven of diamonds. Am I right?

XXXII

'TWAS THE NIGHT BEFORE SUMMER

(An Imaginary Watch-Night with the Weather Man)

IT was 11 o'clock on the night of June 20. We were seated in the office of the Weather Bureau on the twenty-ninth floor of the Whitehall Building, the Weather Man and I, and we were waiting for summer to come. It was officially due on June 21. We had the almanac's word for it and years and years of precedent, but still the Weather Man was skeptical.

It had been a hard spring for the Weather Man. Day after day he had been forced to run a signed statement in the daily papers to the effect that some time during that day there would probably be showers. And day after day, with a ghastly consistency, his prophecy had come true. People had come to dislike him personally; old jokes about him were brought out and oiled and given a trial spin down the road a piece before appearing in funny columns and vaudeville skits, and the sporting writers, frenzied by the task of filling their space with nothing but tables of batting averages, had become positively libellous.

And now summer was at hand, and with it the promise of the sun. The Weather Man nibbled at his thumb nail. The clock on the wall said 11:15.

" It just couldn't go back on us now," he said, plaintively, " when it means so much to us. It always *has* come on the 21st."

There was not much that I could say. I didn't want to hold out any false hope, for I am a child in arms in matters of astronomy, or whatever it is that makes weather.

" I often remember hearing my father tell," I ventured, " how every year on the 21st of June summer always used to come, rain or shine, until they came to look for it on that date, and to count from then as the beginning of the season. It seems as if " ——

" I know," he interrupted, " but there have been so many upsetting things during the past twelve months. We can't check up this year by any other years. All we can do is wait and see."

A gust of wind from Jersey ran along the side of the building, shaking at the windows. The Weather Man shuddered, and looked out of the corner of his eye at the anemometer-register which stood on a table in the middle of the room. It indicated whatever anemometers do indicate when they want to register bad news. I considerately looked out at the window.

" You've no idea," he said at last, in a low voice, " of how this last rainy spell has affected my home life. For the first two or three days, although I got dark looks from slight acquaintances, there was always a cheery welcome waiting for me when I got home, and the Little Woman would say, ' Never mind, Ray, it will soon be pleasant, and we all know that it's not your fault, anyway.'

" But then, after a week had passed and there had been nothing but rain and showers and rain, I began to notice a change. When I would swing in at the gate she would meet me and say, in a far-away voice, ' Well, what is it for to-morrow? ' And I would have to say ' Probably cloudy, with occasional showers and light easterly gales.' At which she would turn away and bite her lip, and once I thought I saw her eye-lashes wet.

" Then, one night, the break came. It had started out to be a perfect day, just such as one reads about, but along about noon it began to cloud over and soon the rain poured down in rain-gauges-full.

She would turn away and bite her lip.

'TWAS THE NIGHT BEFORE SUMMER

" I was all discouraged, and as I wrote out the forecast for the papers, ' Rain to-morrow and Friday,' I felt like giving the whole thing up and going back to Vermont to live.

" When I got home, Alice was there with her things on, waiting for me.

" ' You needn't tell me what it's going to be to-morrow,' she sobbed. ' I know. Every one knows. The whole world knows. I used to think that it wasn't your fault, but when the children come home from school crying because they have been plagued for being the Weather Man's children, when every time I go out I know that the neighbors are talking behind my back and saying " How does she stand it? " when every paper I read, every bulletin I see, stares me in the face with great letters saying, " Weather Man predicts more rain," or " Lynch the Weather Man and let the baseball season go on," then I think it is time for us to come to an understanding. I am going over to mother's until you can do better.' "

The Weather Man got up and went to the window. Out there over the Battery there was a spot casting a sickly glow through the cloud-banks which filled the sky.

" That's the moon up there behind the fog," he said, and laughed a bitter cackle.

LOVE CONQUERS ALL

It was now 11:45. The thermograph was writing busily in red ink on the little diagrammed cuff provided for that purpose, writing all about the temperature. The Weather Man inspected the fine, jagged line as it leaked out of the pen on the chart. Then he walked over to the window again and stood looking out over the bay.

"You'd think that people would have a little gratitude," he said in a low voice, "and not hit at a man who has done so much for them. If it weren't for me where would the art of American conversation be to-day? If there were no weather to talk about, how could there be any dinner parties or church sociables or sidewalk chats?

"All I have to do is put out a real scorcher or a continued cold snap, and I can drive off the boards the biggest news story that was ever launched or draw the teeth out of the most delicate international situation.

"I have saved more reputations and social functions than any other influence in American life, and yet here, when the home office sends me a rummy lot of weather, over which I have no control, everybody jumps on me."

He pulled savagely at the window shade and pressed his nose against the pane in silence for a while.

'TWAS THE NIGHT BEFORE SUMMER

There was no sound but the ticking of the anemometer and the steady scratching of the thermograph. I looked at the clock. 11:47.

Suddenly the telegraph over in the corner snapped like a bunch of firecrackers. In a second the Weather Man was at its side, taking down the message:

" NEW ORLEANS, LA NHRUFKYOTLDMR-ELPWZWOTUDK HEAVY PRECIPITATION SOUTH WESTERLY GALES LETTER FOL-LOWS

NEW ORLEANS U S WEATHER BUREAU

" Poor fellow," muttered the Weather Man, who even in his own tense excitement did not forget the troubles of his brother weather prophet in New Orleans, " I know just how he feels. I hope he's not married."

He glanced at the clock. It was 11:56. In four minutes summer would be due, and with summer a clearer sky, renewed friendships and a united family for the Weather Man. If it failed him — I dreaded to think of what might happen. It was twenty-nine floors to the pavement below, and I am not a powerful man physically.

Together we sat at the table by the thermograph and watched the red line draw mountain ranges along the 50 degree line. From our seats we could look out over the Statue of Liberty and see the cloud-dimmed glow which told of a censored moon. The Weather Man was making nervous little pokes at his collar, as if it had a rough edge that was cutting his neck.

Suddenly he gripped the table. Somewhere a clock was beginning to strike twelve. I shut my eyes and waited.

Ten-eleven-twelve!

" Look, Newspaper Man, look! " he shrieked and grabbed me by the tie.

I opened my eyes and looked at the thermograph. At the last stroke of the clock the red line had given a little, final quaver on the 50 degree line and then had shot up like a rocket until it struck 72 degrees and lay there trembling and heaving like a runner after a race.

But it was not at this that the Weather Man was pointing. There, out in the murky sky, the stroke of twelve had ripped apart the clouds and a large, milk-fed moon was fairly crashing its way through, laying out a straight-away course of silver cinders across the harbor, and in all parts of the heavens stars were breaking out like a rash. In two minutes it had become a balmy, languorous night. Summer had come!

'TWAS THE NIGHT BEFORE SUMMER

I turned to the Weather Man. He was wiping the palms of his hands on his hips and looking foolishly happy. I said nothing. There was nothing that could be said.

Before we left the office he stopped to write out the prophecy for Wednesday, June 21, the First Day of Summer. " Fair and warmer, with slowly rising temperatur." His hand trembled so as he wrote that he forgot the final " e ". Then we went out and he turned toward his home.

On Wednesday, June 21, it rained.

XXXIII

WELCOME HOME — AND SHUT UP!

THERE are a few weeks which bid fair to be pretty trying ones in our national life. They will mark the return to the city of thousands and thousands of vacationists after two months or two weeks of feverish recuperation and there is probably no more obnoxious class of citizen, taken end for end, than the returning vacationist.

In the first place, they are all so offensively healthy. They come crashing through the train-shed, all brown and peeling, as if their health were something they had acquired through some particular credit to themselves. If it were possible, some of them would wear their sun-burned noses on their watch-chains, like Phi Beta Kappa keys.

They have got so used to going about all summer in bathing suits and shirts open at the neck that they look like professional wrestlers in stiff collars and seem to be on the point of bursting out at any minute. And they always make a great deal of noise getting off the train.

"Where's Bessie?" they scream, "Ned, where's

WELCOME HOME — AND SHUT UP!

Bessie? . . . Have you got the thermos bottles?
. . . Well, here's the old station just as it was when
we left it (hysterical laughter). . . . Wallace, you
simply must carry your pail and shovel. Mamma
can't carry *everything*, you know. . . . Mamma
told you that if you wanted to bring your pail and
shovel home you would have to carry it yourself,
don't you remember Mamma told you that, Wallace? . . . Wallace, listen! . . . Edna, have you
got Bessie? . . . Harry's gone after the trunks.
. . . At least, he *said* that was where he was going.
. . . Look, there's the Dexter Building, looking
just the same. Big as life and twice as natural. . . .
I know, Wallace, Mamma's just as hot as you are.
But you don't hear Mamma crying do you? . . . I
wonder where Bert is. . . . He said he'd be down
to meet us sure. . . . Here, give me that cape, Lillian. . . . You're dragging it all over the ground.
. . . *Here's Bert! . . . Whoo-hoo, Bert!* . . .
Here we are! . . . Spencer, there's Daddy! . . .
Whoo-hoo, Daddy! . . . Junior, wipe that gum off
your shoe this minute. . . . *Where's Bessie?* "

And so they go, all the way out into the street
and the cab and home, millions of them. It's
terrible.

And when they get home things are just about as
bad, except there aren't so many people to see them.

LOVE CONQUERS ALL

At the sight of eight Sunday and sixty-two daily papers strewn over the front porch and lawn, there are loud screams of imprecation at Daddy for having forgotten to order them stopped. Daddy insists that he did order them stopped and that it is that damn fool boy.

" I guess you weren't home much during July," says Mamma bitterly, " or you would have noticed that something was wrong." (Daddy didn't join the family until August.)

" There were no papers delivered during July," says Daddy very firmly and quietly, " at least, I didn't see any." (Stepping on one dated July 19.)

The inside of the house resembles some place you might bet a man a hundred dollars he daren't spend the night in. Dead men's feet seem to be protruding from behind sofas and there is a damp smell as if the rooms had been closed pending the arrival of the coroner.

Junior runs upstairs to see if his switching engine is where he left it and comes falling down stairs panting with terror announcing that there is Something in the guest-room. At that moment there is a sound of someone leaving the house by the back door. Daddy is elected by popular vote to go upstairs and see what has happened, although he in-

WELCOME HOME — AND SHUT UP!

sists that he has to wait down stairs as the man with the trunks will be there at any minute. After five minutes of cagey manoeuvering around in the hall outside the guest-room door, he returns looking for Junior, saying that it was simply a pile of things left on the bed covered with a sheet. "Aha-ha-ha-ha-ha!"

Then comes the unpacking. It has been estimated that in the trunks of returning vacationists, taking this section of the country as a whole, the following articles will be pulled out during the next few weeks:

Sneakers, full of sand.

Bathing suits, still damp from the "one last swim."

Dead tennis balls.

Last month's magazines, bought for reading in the grove.

Shells and pretty stones picked up on the beach for decoration purposes, for which there has suddenly become no use at all.

Horse-shoe crabs, salvaged by children who refused to leave them behind.

Lace scarfs and shawls, bought from itinerant Armenians.

Remnants of tubes formerly containing sunburn

[171]

ointment, half-filled bottles of citronella and white shoe-dressing.

White flannel trousers, ready for the cleaners.

Snap-shots, showing Ed and Mollie on the beach in their bathing suits.

Snap-shots which show nothing at all.

Faded flowers, dance-cards and assorted sentimental objects, calculated to bring up tender memories of summer evenings.

Uncompleted knit-sweaters.

Then begins the tour of the neighborhood, comparing summer-vacation experiences. To each returning vacationist it seems as if everyone in town must be interested in what he or she did during the summer. They stop perfect strangers on the streets and say: " Well, a week ago today at this time we were all walking up to the Post-Office for the mail. Right out in front of the Post-Office were the fish-houses and you ought to have seen Billy one night leading a lobster home on a string. That was the night we all went swimming by moon-light."

" Yeah? " says the stranger, and pushes his way past.

Then two people get together who have been to different places. Neither wants to hear about the other's summer — and neither does. Both talk at once and pull snap-shots out of their pockets.

" Here's where we used to take our lunch — "

"That's nothing. Steve had a friend up the lake who had a launch — "

"—and everyday there was something doing over at the Casino — "

" — and you ought to have seen Miriam, she was a sight — "

Pretty soon they come to blows trying to make each other listen. The only trouble is they never quite kill each other. If only one could be killed it would be a great help.

The next ban on immigration should be on returning vacationists. Have government officials stationed in each city and keep everyone out who won't give a bond to shut up and go right to work.

XXXIV

ANIMAL STORIES

I

How Georgie Dog Gets the Rubbers on the Guest Room Bed

OLD Mother Nature gathered all her little pupils about her for the daily lesson in " How the Animals Do the Things They Do." Every day Waldo Lizard, Edna Elephant and Lawrence Walrus came to Mother Nature's school, and there learned all about the useless feats performed by their brother and sister animals.

" Today," said Mother Nature, " we shall find out how it is that Georgie Dog manages to get the muddy rubbers from the hall closet, up the stairs, and onto the nice white bedspread in the guest room. You must be sure to listen carefully and pay strict attention to what Georgie Dog says. Only, don't take too much of it seriously, for Georgie is an awful liar."

And, sure enough, in came Georgie Dog, wagging his entire torso in a paroxysm of camaradarie, although everyone knew that he had no use for Waldo Lizard.

" Tell us, Georgie," said Mother Nature, " how do you do your clever work of rubber-dragging? We would like so much to know. Wouldn't we, children? "

" No, Mother Nature! " came the instant response from the children.

So Georgie Dog began.

" Well, I'll tell you; it's this way," he said, snapping at a fly. " You have to be very niftig about it. First of all, I lie by the door of the hall closet until I see a nice pair of muddy rubbers kicked into it."

" How muddy ought they to be? " asked Edna Elephant, although little enough use she would have for the information.

" I am glad that you asked that question," replied Georgie. " Personally, I like to have mud on them about the consistency of gurry — that is, not too wet — because then it will all drip off on the way upstairs, and not so dry that it scrapes off on the carpet. For we must save it all for the bedspread, you know.

" As soon as the rubbers are safely in the hall closet, I make a great deal of todo about going into the other room, in order to give the impression

that there is nothing interesting enough in the hall
to keep me there. A good, loud yawn helps to
disarm any suspicion of undue excitement. I sometimes even chew a bit of fringe on the sofa and take
a scolding for it — anything to draw attention from
the rubbers. Then, when everyone is at dinner, I
sneak out and drag them forth."

"And how do you manage to take them both at
once?" piped up Lawrence Walrus.

"I am glad that you asked that question," said
Georgie, "because I was trying to avoid it. You
can never guess what the answer is. It is very
difficult to take two at a time, and so we usually
have to take one and then go back and get the
other. I had a cousin once who knew a grip which
could be worked on the backs of overshoes, by
means of which he could drag two at a time, but
he was an exceptionally fine dragger. He once
took a pair of rubber boots from the barn into the
front room, where a wedding was taking place, and
put them on the bride's train. Of course, not one
dog in a million could hope to do that.

"Once upstairs, it is quite easy getting them into
the guest room, unless the door happens to be shut.
Then what do you think I do? I go around
through the bathroom window onto the roof, and
walk around to the sleeping porch, and climb down

into the guest room that way. It is a lot of trouble, but I think that you will agree with me that the results are worth it.

" Climbing up on the bed with the rubbers in my mouth is difficult, but it doesn't make any difference if some of the mud comes off on the side of the bedspread. In fact, it all helps in the final effect. I usually try to smear them around when I get them at last on the spread, and if I can leave one of them on the pillow, I feel that it's a pretty fine little old world, after all. This done, and I am off."

And Georgie Dog suddenly disappeared in official pursuit of an automobile going eighty-five miles an hour.

" So now," said Mother Nature to her little pupils, " we have heard all about Georgie Dog's work. To-morrow we may listen to Lillian Mosquito tell how she makes her voice carry across a room."

ANIMAL STORIES

II

How Lillian Mosquito Projects Her Voice

ALL the children came crowding around Mother Nature one cold, raw afternoon in summer, crying in unison:

"Oh, Mother Nature, you promised us that you would tell us how Lillian Mosquito projects her voice! You promised that you would tell us how Lillian Mosquito projects her voice!"

"So I did! So I did!" said Mother Nature, laying down an oak, the leaves of which she was tipping with scarlet for the fall trade. "And so I will! So I will!"

At which Waldo Lizard, Edna Elephant and Lawrence Walrus jumped with imitation joy, for they had hoped to have an afternoon off.

Mother Nature led them across the fields to the piazza of a clubhouse on which there was an exposed ankle belonging to one of the members. There, as she had expected, they found Lillian Mosquito having tea.

"Lillian," called Mother Nature, "come off a minute. I have some little friends here who would like to know how it is that you manage to hum in such a manner as to give the impression of being just outside the ear of a person in bed, when actually you are across the room."

" Will you kindly repeat the question? " said Lillian flying over to the railing.

" We want to know," said Mother Nature, " how it is that very often, when you have been fairly caught, it turns out that you have escaped without injury."

" I would prefer to answer the question as it was first put," said Lillian.

So Waldo Lizard, Edna Elephant and Lawrence Walrus, seeing that there was no way out, cried:

" Yes, yes, Lillian, do tell us."

" First of all, you must know," began Lillian Mosquito, " that my chief duty is to annoy. Whatever else I do, however many bites I total in the course of the evening, I do not consider that I have ' made good ' unless I have caused a great deal of annoyance while doing it. A bite, quietly executed and not discovered by the victim until morning, does me no good. It is my duty, and my pleasure, to play with him before biting, as you have often heard a cat plays with a mouse, tormenting him with apprehension and making him struggle to defend himself. . . . If I am using too long words for you, please stop me."

LOVE CONQUERS ALL

"Stop!" cried Waldo Lizard, reaching for his hat, with the idea of possibly getting to the ball park by the fifth inning.

But he was prevented from leaving by kindly old Mother Nature, who stepped on him with her kindly old heel, and Lillian Mosquito continued:

"I must therefore, you see, be able to use my little voice with great skill. Of course, the first thing to do is to make my victim think that I am nearer to him than I really am. To do this, I sit quite still, let us say, on the footboard of the bed, and, beginning to hum in a very, very low tone of voice, increase the volume and raise the pitch gradually, thereby giving the effect of approaching the pillow.

"The man in bed thinks that he hears me coming toward his head, and I can often see him, waiting with clenched teeth until he thinks that I am near enough to swat. Sometimes I strike a quick little grace-note, as if I were right above him and about to make a landing. It is great fun at such times to see him suddenly strike himself over the ear (they always think that I am right at their ear), and then feel carefully between his finger tips to see if he has caught me. Then, too, there is always the pleasure of thinking that perhaps he has hurt himself quite badly by the blow. I have often known victims of mine to deafen themselves permanently by jarring their eardrums in their wild attempts to catch me."

"What fun! What fun!" cried Edna Elephant. "I must try it myself just as soon as ever I get home."

"It is often a good plan to make believe that you have been caught after one of the swats," continued Lillian Mosquito, "and to keep quiet for a while. It makes him cocky. He thinks that he has demonstrated the superiority of man over the rest of the animals. Then he rolls over and starts to sleep. This is the time to begin work on him again. After he has slapped himself all over the face and head, and after he has put on the light and made a search of the room and then gone back to bed to think up some new words, that is the time when I usually bring the climax about.

"Gradually approaching him from the right, I hum loudly at his ear. Then, suddenly becoming quiet, I fly silently and quickly around to his neck. Just as he hits himself on the ear, I bite his neck and fly away. And, *voilà*, there you are!"

"How true that is!" said Mother Nature. "*Voilà*, there we are! . . . Come, children, let us go now, for we must be up bright and early to-morrow to learn how Lois Hen scratches up the beets and Swiss chard in the gentlemen's gardens."

XXXV

THE TARIFF UNMASKED

LET us get this tariff thing cleared up, once and for all. An explanation is due the American people, and obviously this is the place to make it.

Viewing the whole thing, schedule by schedule, we find it indefensible. In Schedule A alone the list of necessities on which the tax is to be raised includes Persian berries, extract of nutgalls and isinglass. Take isinglass alone. With prices shooting up in this market, what is to become of our picture post-cards? Where once for a nickel you could get a picture of the Woolworth Building ablaze with lights with the sun setting and the moon rising in the background, under the proposed tariff it will easily set you back fifteen cents. This is all very well for the rich who can get their picture post-cards at wholesale, but how are the poor to get their art?

The only justifiable increase in this schedule is on " blues, in pulp, dried, etc." If this will serve to reduce the amount of " Those

Lonesome-Onesome-Wonesome Blues " and " I've Got the Left-All-Alone-in-The-Magazine-Reading-Room-of-the-Public-Library Blues " with which our popular song market has been flooded for the past five years, we could almost bring ourselves to vote for the entire tariff bill as it stands.

Schedule B

Here we find a tremendous increase in the tax on grindstones. Householders and travelers in general do not appreciate what this means. It means that, next year, when you are returning from Europe, you will have to pay a duty on those Dutch grindstones that you always bring back to the cousins, a duty which will make the importation of more than three prohibitive. This will lead to an orgy of grindstone smuggling, making it necessary for hitherto respectable people to become law-breakers by concealing grindstones about their clothing and in the trays of their trunks. Think this over.

Schedule C

Right at the start of this list we find charcoal bars being boosted. Have our children no rights? What is a train-ride with children without Hershey's charcoal bars? Or gypsum? What more picturesque on a ride through the country-side than a band of gypsum encamped by the road with their bright colors and gay tambourine playing? Are these simple folk to be kept out of this country simply because a Republican tariff insists on raising the tax on gypsum?

Schedule D

A way to evade the injustice of this schedule is in the matter of marble slabs. " Marble slabs, rubbed " are going to cost more to import than " marble slabs, unrubbed." What we are planning to do in this office is to get in a quantity of unrubbed marble slabs and then rub them ourselves. A coarse, dry towel is very good for rubbing, they say.

Any further discussion of the details of this iniquitous tariff would only enrage us to a point of incoherence. Perhaps a short list of some of the things you will have to do without under the new arrangement will serve to enrage you also:

Senegal gum, buchu leaves, lava tips for burners, magic lantern strips, spiegeleisen nut washers, butchers' skewers and gun wads.

Now write to your congressman!

LITERARY DEPARTMENT

XXXVI

"TAKE ALONG A BOOK"

THERE seems to be a concerted effort, manifest in the "Take Along a Book" drive, to induce vacationists to slip at least one volume into the trunk before getting Daddy to jump on it.

This is a fine idea, for there is always a space between the end of the tennis-racquet and the box of soap in which the shoe-whitening is liable to tip over unless you jam a book in with it. Any book will do.

It is usually a book that you have been meaning to read all Spring, one that you have got so used to lying about to people who have asked you if you have read it that you have almost kidded yourself into believing that you really have read it. You picture yourself out in the hammock or down on the rocks, with a pillow under your head and pipe or a box of candy near at hand, just devouring page after page of it. The only thing that worries you is what you will read when you have finished that. "Oh, well," you think, "there will probably be some books in the town library. Maybe I can get

Gibbon there. This summer will be a good time to read Gibbon through."

Your trunk doesn't reach the cottage until four days after you arrive, owing to the ferry-pilots' strike. You don't get it unpacked down as far as the layer in which the book is until you have been there a week.

Then the book is taken out and put on the table. In transit it has tried to eat its way through a pair of tramping-boots, with the result that one corner and the first twenty pages have become dog-eared, but that won't interfere with its being read.

Several other things do interfere, however. The nice weather, for instance. You start out from your room in the morning and somehow or other never get back to it except when you are in a hurry to get ready for meals or for bed. You try to read in bed one night, but you can't seem to fix your sunburned shoulders in a comfortable position.

You take the book down to luncheon and leave it at the table. And you don't miss it for three days. When you find it again it has large blisters on page 35 where some water was dropped on it.

Then Mrs. Beatty, who lives in Montclair in the winter time (no matter where you go for the summer, you always meet some people who live in Montclair in the winter), borrows the book, as she has heard so much about it. Two weeks later she brings it back, and explains that Prince got hold of it one afternoon and chewed just a little of the back off, but says that she doesn't think it will be noticed when the book is in the bookcase.

Back to the table in the bedroom it goes and is used to keep unanswered post-cards in. It also is convenient as a backing for cards which you yourself are writing. And the flyleaf makes an excellent place for a bridge-score if there isn't any other paper handy.

When it comes time to pack up for home, you shake the sand from among the leaves and save out the book to be read on the train. And you leave it in the automobile that takes you to the station.

But for all that, " take along a book." It might rain all summer.

XXXVII

CONFESSIONS OF A CHESS
CHAMPION

WITH the opening of the baseball season, the
sporting urge stirs in one's blood and we
turn to such books as " My Chess Career," by J. R.
Capablanca. Mr. Capablanca, I gather from his
text, plays chess very well. Wherein he unquestionably has something on me.

His book is a combination of autobiography and
pictorial examples of difficult games he has partici-
pated in and won. I could understand the autobi-
ographical part perfectly, but although I have seen
chess diagrams in the evening papers for years, I
never have been able to become nervous over one.
It has always seemed to me that when you have
seen one diagram of a chessboard you have seen
them all. Therefore, I can give only a superficial
review of the technical parts of Mr. Capablanca's
book.

His personal reminiscences, however, are full of
poignant episodes. For instance, let us take an

incident which occurred in his early boyhood when he found out what sort of man his father really was — a sombre event in the life of any boy, much more so for the boy Capablanca.

" I was born in Havana, the capital of the Island of Cuba," he says, " the 19th of November, 1888. I was not yet five years old when by accident I came into my father's private office and found him playing with another gentleman. I had never seen a game of chess before; the pieces interested me and I went the next day to see them play again. The third day, as I looked on, my father, a very poor beginner, moved a Knight from a white square to another white square. His opponent, apparently not a better player, did not notice it. My father won, and I proceeded to call him a cheat and to laugh."

Imagine the feelings of a young boy entering his father's private office and seeing a man whom he had been brought up to love and to revere moving a Knight from one white square to another. It is a wonder that the boy had the courage to grow up at all with a start in life like that.

But he did grow up, and at the age of eight, in spite of the advice of doctors, he was a frequent visitor at the Havana Chess Club. As he says in describing this period of his career, " Soon Don Celso Golmayo, the strongest player there, was unable to give me a rook." So you can see how good he was. Don Celso couldn't give him a rook. And if Don Celso couldn't, who on earth could?

In his introduction, Mr. Capablanca (I wish that I could get it out of my head that Mr. Capablanca is possibly a relation of the Casabianca boy who did the right thing by the burning deck. They are, of course, two entirely different people) — in his introduction, Mr. Capablanca says:

" Conceit I consider a foolish thing; but more foolish still is that false modesty that vainly attempts to conceal that which all facts tend to prove."

It is this straining to overcome a foolish, false modesty which leads him to say, in connection with his matches with members of the Manhattan Chess Club. " As one by one I mowed them down without the loss of a single game, my superiority became apparent." Or, in speaking of his " endings " (a term we chess experts use to designate the last part of our game), to murmur modestly: " The endings I already played very well, and to my mind had attained the high standard for which they were in the future to be well known." Mr. Capablanca will have to watch that false modesty of his. It will get him into trouble some day.

CONFESSIONS OF A CHESS CHAMPION

Although this column makes no pretense of carrying sporting news, it seems only right to print a part of the running story of the big game between Capablanca and Dr. O. S. Bernstein in the San Sebastian tournament of 1911. Capablanca wore the white, while Dr. Bernstein upheld the honor of the black.

The tense moment of the game had been reached. Capablanca has the ball on Dr. Bernstein's 3-yard line on the second down, with a minute and a half to play. The stands are wild. Cries of "Hold 'em, Bernstein!" and "Touchdown, Capablanca!" ring out on the frosty November air.

Brave voices are singing the fighting song entitled "Capablanca's Day" which runs as follows:

> "Oh, sweep, sweep across the board,
>   With your castles, queens, and pawns;
>   We are with you, all Havana's horde,
>   Till the sun of victory dawns;
>   Then it's fight, *fight*, FIGHT!
>   To your last white knight,
>   For the truth must win alway,
>   And our hearts beat true
>   Old "J. R." for you
>   On Capa-blanca's Day."

LOVE CONQUERS ALL

" Up to this point the game had proceeded along the lines generally recommended by the masters," writes Capablanca. " The last move, however, is a slight deviation from the regular course, which brings this Knight back to B in order to leave open the diagonal for the Q, and besides is more in accordance with the defensive nature of the game. Much more could be said as to the reasons that make Kt - B the preferred move of most masters. . . . Of course, lest there be some misapprehension, let me state that the move Kt - B is made in conjunction with K R - K, which comes first."

It is lucky that Mr. Casabianca made that explanation, for I was being seized with just that misapprehension which he feared. (Mr. *Capablanca*, I mean.)

Below is the box-score by innings:

1.	P - K4.	P - K4.
2.	Kt - QB3.	Kt - QB3.
3.	P - B4.	P x P.
4.	Kt - B3.	P - K Kt4.

(Game called on account of darkness.)

XXXVIII

"RIP VAN WINKLE"

AFTER all, there is nothing like a good folk-
opera for wholesome fun, and the boy who
can turn out a rollicking folk-opera for old and
young is Percy MacKaye. His latest is a riot from
start to finish. You can buy it in book form, published by Knopf. Just ask for " Rip Van Winkle "
and spend the evening falling out of your chair.
(You wake up just as soon as you fall and are all
ready again for a fresh start.)

Of course it is a little rough in spots, but you
know what Percy MacKaye is when he gets loose
on a folk-opera. It is good, clean Rabelaisian fun,
such as was in " Washington, the Man Who Made
Us." I always felt that it was very prudish of the
police to stop that play just as it was commencing
its run. Or maybe it wasn't the police that stopped
it. Something did, I remember.

But " Rip Van Winkle " has much more zip to it
than " Washington " had. In the first place, the
lyrics are better. They have more of a lilt to them
than the lines of the earlier work had. Here is the

song hit of the first act, sung by the Goose Girl.
Try this over on your piano:

> *Kaaterskill, Kaaterskill,*
> *Cloud on the Kaaterskill!*
> *Will it be fair, or lower?*
> *Silver rings*
> *On my pond I see;*
> *And my gander he*
> *Shook both his white wings*
> *Like a sunshine shower.*

I venture to say that Irving Berlin himself
couldn't have done anything catchier than that by
way of a lyric. Or this little snatch of a refrain
sung by the old women of the town:

> *Nay, nay, nay!*
> *A sunshine shower*
> *Won't last a half an hour.*

The trouble with most lyrics is that they are written by song-writers who have had no education. Mr.
MacKaye's college training shows itself in every
line of the opera. There is a sublety of rhyme-
scheme, a delicacy of metre, and, above all, an
originality of thought and expression which prom-
ises much for the school of university-bred lyricists·

" RIP VAN WINKLE "

Here, for instance, is a lyric which Joe McCarthy could never have written:

Up spoke Nancy, spanking Nancy,
Says, " My feet are far too dancy, Dancy O!
So foot-on-the-grass,
Foot-on-the-grass,
Foot-on-the-grass is my fancy, O! "

Of course this is a folk-opera. And you can get away with a great deal of that " dancy-o " stuff when you call it a folk-opera. You can throw it all back on the old folk at home and they can't say a word.

But even the local wits of Rip Van Winkle's time would have repudiated the comedy lines which Mr. MacKaye gives Rip to say in which " Katy-did " and " Katy-didn't " figure prominently as the nub, followed, before you have time to stop laughing, by one about " whip poor Will " (whippoorwill — get it?). If " Rip Van Winkle " is ever produced again, Ed Wynn should be cast as Rip. He would eat that line alive.

Ed Wynn, by the way, might do wonders by the opera if he could get the rights to produce it in his own way. Let Mr. MacKaye's name stay on the programme, but give Ed Wynn the white card to do as he might see fit with the book. For instance, one of Mr. MacKaye's characters is named " Dirck Spuytenduyvil." Let him stand as he is, but give him two cousins, " Mynheer Yonkers " and " Jan One Hundred and Eighty-third Street." The three of them could do a comedy tumbling act. There is practically no end to the features that could be introduced to tone the thing up.

The basic idea of " Rip Van Winkle " would lend itself admirably to Broadway treatment, for Mr. MacKaye has taken liberties, with the legend and introduced the topical idea of a Magic Flask, containing home-made hootch. Hendrick Hudson, the Captain of the Catskill Bowling Team, is the lucky possessor of the doctor's prescription and formula, and it is in order to take a trial spin with the brew that Rip first goes up to the mountain. Here are Hendrick's very words of invitation:

You'll be right welcome. I will let you taste
A wonder drink we brew aboard the Half Moon.
Whoever drinks the Magic Flask thereof
Forgets all lapse of time
And wanders ever in the fairy season
Of youth and spring.
Come join me in the mountains
At mid of night
And there I promise you the Magic Flask.

And so at mid of night Rip fell for the promise of wandering " in the fairy season," as so many have done at the invitation of a man who has " made a little something at home which you couldn't tell from the real stuff." Rip got out of it easily. He simply went to sleep for twenty years. You ought to see a man I know.

There is a note in the front of the volume saying that no public reading of " Rip Van Winkle " may be given without first getting the author's permission. It ought to be made much more difficult to do than that.

XXXIX

LITERARY LOST AND FOUND
DEPARTMENT

With Scant Apology to the Book Section of the
New York Times.

"Old Black Tillie"

H.G.L. — When I was a little girl, my nurse used to recite a poem something like the following (as near as I can remember). I wonder if anyone can give me the missing lines?

"Old Black Tillie lived in the dell,
Heigh-ho with a rum-tum-tum!
Something, something, something like a lot of hell,
Heigh-ho with a rum-tum-tum!
She wasn't very something and she wasn't very
fat
But — "

"Victor Hugo's Death"

M.K.C. — Is it true that Victor Hugo did not die but is still living in a little shack in Colorado?

LITERARY LOST AND FOUND

"I'm Sorry That I Spelt the Word"

J.R.A. — Can anyone help me out by furnishing the last three words to the following stanza which I learned in school and of which I have forgotten the last three words, thereby driving myself crazy?

> "' I'm sorry that I spelt the word,
> I hate to go above you,
> Because —' the brown eyes lower fell,
> ' Because, you see, — — — .'"

"God's in His Heaven"

J.A.E. — Where did Mark Twain write the following?

> " God's in his heaven:
> All's right with the world."

"She Dwelt Beside"

N.K.Y. — Can someone locate this for me and tell the author?

> " She dwelt among untrodden ways,
> Beside the springs of Dove,
> To me she gave sweet Charity,
> But greater far is Love."

LOVE CONQUERS ALL

"The Golden Wedding"

K.L.F. — Who wrote the following and what does it mean?

> " *Oh, de golden wedding,*
> *Oh, de golden wedding,*
> *Oh, de golden wedding,*
> *De golden, golden wedding!* "

ANSWERS

"When Grandma Was a Girl"

Luther F. Neam, Flushing, L. I. — The poem asked for by " E.J.K." was recited at a Free Soil riot in Ashburg, Kansas, in July, 1850. It was entitled, " And That's the Way They Did It When Grandma Was a Girl," and was written by Bishop Leander B. Rizzard. The last line runs:

> " *And that's they way they did it, when Grandma*
> *was a girl.*"

Others who answered this query were: Lillian W. East, of Albany; Martin B. Forsch, New York City, and Henry Cabot Lodge, Nahant.

LITERARY LOST AND FOUND

"Let Us Then Be Up and Doing"

Roger F. Nilkette, Presto, N.J. — Replying to the query in your last issue concerning the origin of the lines:

> *" Let us then be up and doing,*
> *With a heart for any fate.*
> *Still achieving, still pursuing,*
> *Learn to labor and to wait."*

I remember hearing these lines read at a gathering in the Second Baptist Church of Presto, N. J., when I was a young man, by the Reverend Harley N. Ankle. It was said at the time among his parishioners that he himself wrote them and on being questioned on the matter he did not deny it, simply smiling and saying, " I'm glad if you liked them." They were henceforth known in Presto as " Dr. Ankle's verse " and were set to music and sung at his funeral.

"The December Bride, or Old Robin"

Charles B. Rennit, Boston, N. H. — The whole poem wanted by " H.J.O." is as follows, and appeared in *Hostetter's Annual* in 1843.

LOVE CONQUERS ALL

1

" 'Twas in the bleak December that I took her for
*   my bride;*
How well do I remember how she fluttered by my
*   side;*
My Nellie dear, it was not long before you up and
*   died,*
And they buried her at eight-thirty in the morning.

2

" Oh, do not tell me of the charms of maidens far
*   and near,*
Their charming ways and manners I do not care to
*   hear,*
For Lucy dear was to me so very, very dear,
And they buried her at eight-thirty in the morning.

3

" Then it's merrily, merrily, merrily, whoa!
To the old gray church they come and go,
Some to be married and some to be buried,
And old Robin has gone for the mail."

" THE OLD KING'S JOKE "

F. J. BRUFF, Hammick, Conn. — In a recent issue
of your paper, Lillian F. Grothman asked for the

remainder of a poem which began: *"The King of Sweden made a joke, ha, ha!"*

I can furnish all of this poem, having written it myself, for which I was expelled from St. Domino's School in 1895. If Miss Grothman will meet me in the green room at the Biltmore for tea on Wednesday next at 4:30, she will be supplied with the missing words.

XL

" DARKWATER "

WE have so many, many problems in America.
Books are constantly being written offering
solutions for them, but still they persist.

There are volumes on auction bridge, family
budgets and mind-training. A great many people
have ideas on what should be done to relieve the
country of certain undesirable persons who have
displayed a lack of sympathy with American institutions. (As if American institutions needed sympathy!) And some of the more generous-minded
among us are writing books showing our duty to
the struggling young nationalities of Europe. It
is bewildering to be confronted by all these problems, each demanding intelligent solution.

Little wonder, then, that we have no time for
writing books on the one problem which is exclusively our own. With so many wrongs in the world
to be righted, who can blame us for overlooking
the one tragic wrong which lies at our door? With
so many heathen to whom the word of God must be

brought and so many wild revolutionists in whom must be instilled a respect for law and order, is it strange that we should ourselves sometimes lump the word of God and the principles of law and order together under the head of " sentimentality " and shrug our shoulders? Justice in the abstract is our aim — any American will tell you that — so why haggle over details and insist on justice for the negro?

But W. E. B. Du Bois does insist on justice for the negro, and in his book " Darkwater " (Harcourt, Brace & Co.) his voice rings out in a bitter warning through the complacent quiet which usually reigns around this problem of America. Mr. Du Bois seems to forget that we have the affairs of a great many people to attend to and persists in calling our attention to this affair of our own. And what is worse, in the minds of all well-bred persons he does not do it at all politely. He seems to be quite distressed about something.

Maybe it is because he finds himself, a man of superior mind and of sensitive spirit who is a graduate of Harvard, a professor and a sincere worker for the betterment of mankind, relegated to an inferior order by many men and women who are obviously his inferiors, simply because he happens

to differ from them in the color of his skin. Maybe
it is because he sees the people of his own race who
have not had his advantages (if a negro may ever
be said to have received an advantage) being
crowded into an ignominious spiritual serfdom
equally as bad as the physical serfdom from
which they were so recently freed. Maybe it is
because of these things that Mr. Du Bois seems
overwrought.

Or perhaps it is because he reads each day of
how jealous we are, as a Nation, of the sanctity of
our Constitution, how we revere it and draw a flash-
ing sword against its detractors, and then sees this
very Constitution being flouted as a matter of course
in those districts where the amendment giving the
negroes a right to vote is popularly considered one
of the five funniest jokes in the world.

Perhaps he hears candidates for office insisting on
a reign of law or a plea for order above all things,
by some sentimentalist or other, or public speakers
advising those who have not respect for American
institutions to go back whence they came, and then
sees whole sections of the country violating every
principle of law and order and mocking American
institutions for the sake of teaching a " nigger "
his place.

"DARKWATER"

Perhaps during the war he heard of the bloody crimes of our enemies, and saw preachers and editors and statesmen stand aghast at the barbaric atrocities which won for the German the name of Hun, and then looked toward his own people and saw them being burned, disembowelled and tortured with a civic unanimity and tacit legal sanction which made the word Hun sound weak.

Perhaps he has heard it boasted that in America every man who is honest, industrious and intelligent has a good chance to win out, and has seen honest, industrious and intelligent men whose skins are black stopped short by a wall so high and so thick that all they can do, on having reached that far, is to bow their heads and go slowly back.

Any one of these reasons should have been sufficient for having written " Darkwater."

It is unfortunate that Mr. Du Bois should have raised this question of our own responsibility just at this time when we were showing off so nicely. It may remind some one that instead of taking over a protectorate of Armenia we might better take over a protectorate of the State of Georgia, which yearly leads the proud list of lynchers. But then, there will not be enough people who see Mr. Du Bois's book to cause any great national movement, so we are quite sure, for the time being, of being able to devote our energies to the solution of our other problems.

Don't forget, therefore, to write your Congressman about a universal daylight-saving bill, and give a little thought, if you can, to the question of the vehicular tunnel.

XLI

THE NEW TIME–TABLE

THE new time-table of the New York Central Railroad (New York Central Railroad, Harlem Division. Form 113. Corrected to March 28, 1922) is an attractive folder, done in black and white, for the suburban trade. It slips neatly into the pocket, where it easily becomes lost among letters and bills, appearing again only when you have procured another.

So much for its physical features. Of the text matter it is difficult to write without passion. No more disheartening work has been put on the market this season.

In an attempt to evade the Daylight-Saving Law the New York Central has kept its clocks at what is called " Eastern Standard Time," meaning that it is standard on East 42d Street between Vanderbilt and Lexington Avenues. Practically everywhere else in New York the clocks are an hour ahead.

It is this " Eastern Standard Time " that gives the time-table its distinctive flavor. Each train has been demoted one hour, and then, for fear that it would be too easy to understand this, an extra three or four minutes have been thrown in or taken out, just so that no mistake can help being made.

In order to read the new time-table understandingly the following procedure is now necessary:

Take a room in some quiet family hotel where the noise from the street is reduced to minimum. Place the time-table on the writing-desk and sit in front of it, holding a pencil in the right hand and a watch (Eastern Christian Time) in the left. Then decide on the time you think you would like to reach home. Let us say that you usually have dinner at 7. You would, if you could do just what you wanted, reach Valhalla at 6:30. Very well. It takes about an hour from the Grand Central Terminal to Valhalla. How about a train leaving around 5:30?

Look at the time-table for a train which leaves about 2:45 (Eastern Standard Time). Write down, " 2:45 " on a piece of paper. Add 150. Subtract the number of stations that Valhalla is above White Plains. Sharpen your pencil and bind up your cut finger and subtract the number you first thought of, and the result will show the number of Presidents of the United States who have been assassinated while in office. Then go over to the Grand Central

"Listen, Ed! This is how it goes!"

Terminal and ask one of the information clerks what you want to know.

They will be glad to see you, for during the last three days they have been actually hungering for the sight of a human face. Sometimes it has seemed to them that the silence and loneliness there behind the information counter would drive them mad. If some one — any one — would only come and speak to them! That is why one of them is over in the corner chewing up time-tables into small balls and playing marbles with them. He has gone mad from loneliness. The other clerk, the one who is looking at the tip of his nose and mumbling Lincoln's Gettysburg Address, has only a few more minutes before he too succumbs.

And that low, rumbling sound, what is that? It comes from the crowd of commuters standing in front of the gate of what used to be the 5:56. Let us draw near and. hear what they are discussing. Why, it is the new time-table, of all things!

"Listen, Ed. This is how it goes. This train that goes at 4:25 according to this time-table is really the old 5:20. See? What you do is add an hour " ——

"Aw, what kind of talk is that? Add an hour to your grandmother! You subtract an hour from the time as given here. This is Eastern Standard Time. See, it says right here: ' The time shown in this folder is Eastern Standard Time, one hour slower than Daylight-Saving Time.' See? One hour slower. You subtract."

"Here, you guys are both way off. I just asked one of the trainmen. The 5:56 has gone. It went at 4:20. The next train that we get is the 6:20 which goes at 5:19. Look, see here. It says 5:19 on the time-table but that means that by your watch it is 6:19 " ——

" By my watch it is not 6:19. My watch I set by the clock in the station this morning when I came in " ——

" Well, the clock in the station is wrong. That is, the clock in the station is an hour ahead of all the other clocks."

" An hour ahead? An hour behind, you mean."

" The clock in the station is an hour ahead. I know what I'm talking about."

" Now listen, Jo. Didn't you see in the paper Monday morning " ——

" Yaas, I saw in the paper Monday morning, and it said that "——

" Look, Gus. By my watch — look, Gus — listen, Gus — by my watch " ——

THE NEW TIME–TABLE

" Aw, you and your watch!   What's that got to do with it? "

" Now   looka   here.   On   this   time-table   it says " ——

" Lissen, Eddie " ——

Whatever else its publishers may say about it, the new New York Central time-table bids fair to be the most-talked-of publication of the season.

XLII

MR. BOK'S AMERICANIZATION

IF ever you should feel important enough to write an autobiography to give to the world, and dislike to say all the nice things about yourself that you feel really ought to be said, just write it in the third person. Edward Bok has done this in " The Americanization of Edward Bok " and the effect is quite touching in its modesty.

In " An Explanation " at the beginning of the book Mr. Bok disclaims any credit for the winning ways and remarkable success of his hero, Edward Bok. Edward Bok, the little Dutch boy who landed in America in 1870 and later became the editor of the greatest women's advertising medium in the country, is an entirely different person from the Edward Bok who is telling the story. You understand this to begin with. Otherwise you may misjudge the author.

" I have again and again found myself," writes Mr. Bok, " watching with intense amusement and interest the Edward Bok of this book at work. . . . His tastes, his outlook, his manner of looking at

MR. BOK'S AMERICANIZATION
things were totally at variance with my own. . . .
He has had and has been a personality apart from
my private self."

The only connection between Edward Bok the
editor and Edward Bok the autobiographer seems
to be that Editor Bok allows Author Bok to have
a checking account in his bank under their common
name.

Thus completely detached from his hero, Mr. Bok
proceeds and is able to narrate on page 3, in the
manner of Horatio Alger, how young Edward,
taunted by his Brooklyn schoolmates, gave a sound
thrashing to the ringleader, after which he found
himself " looking into the eyes of a crowd of very
respectful boys and giggling girls, who readily made
a passageway for his brother and himself when they
indicated a desire to leave the school-yard and go
home."

He can also, without seeming in the least conceited,
tell how, through his clear-sighted firmness in refusing to write in the Spencerian manner prescribed in
school, he succeeded in bringing the Principal and
the whole Board of Education to their senses, resulting in a complete reversal of the public-school policy
in the matter of handwriting instruction.

The Horatio Alger note is dominant throughout
the story of young Edward's boyhood. His cheer-

fulness and business sagacity so impressed everyone with whom he came in contact that he was soon outdistancing all the other boys in the process of self-advancement. And no one is more smilingly tolerant of the irresistible progress of young Edward Bok in making friends and money than Edward Bok the impersonal author of the book. He just loves to see the young boy get ahead.

It will perhaps aid in getting an idea of the personality and confident presence of the Boy Bok to state that he was a feverish collector of autographs. Whenever any famous personage came to town the young man would find out at what hotel he was staying and would proceed to hound him until he had got him to write his name, with some appropriate sentiment, in a little book. In advertising the present volume the publishers give a list of names of historical characters who feature in Mr. Bok's reminiscences — Gens. Grant and Garfield, Oliver Wendell Holmes, Longfellow, Emerson and dozens of others. And so they do figure in the book, but as victims of the young Dutch boy's passion for autographs. Still, perhaps, they did not mind, for the author gives us to understand that they were all so charmed with the prepossessing manner and intelligent bearing of the young autograph hound that they not only were continually asking him to dinner (he usually timed his visit so as to catch them just as they were entering the dining-room) but insisted on giving him letters of introduction to their friends.

Only Mrs. Abraham Lincoln and Ralph Waldo Emerson neglected to register extreme pleasure at being approached by the smiling lad. Both Mrs. Lincoln and Emerson were failing in their minds at the time, however, which satisfactorily explains their coolness, at least for the author. In Mrs. Lincoln's case an attempt was made to interest her in an autographed photograph of Gen. Grant. But " Edward saw that the widow of the great Lincoln did not mentally respond to his pleasure in his possession." Could it have been possible that the widow of the great Lincoln was a trifle bored?

The account of the intrusion on Emerson in Concord borders on the sacrilegious. Here was the venerable philosopher, five months before his death, when his great mind had already gone on before him, being visited by a strange lad with a passion for autographs, who sat and watched for those lucid moments when the sun would break through the clouded brain, making it possible for Emerson to hold the pen and form the letters of his name. Then young Edward was off, with another trophy in his belt and another stride made in his progress toward

LOVE CONQUERS ALL

Americanization. Lovers of Emerson could wish
that the impersonal editor of these memoirs had
omitted the account of this victory.

Americanization seems, from the present docu-
ment, to consist of, first, making as many influential
friends as possible who may be able to help you at
some future time; second, making as much money
as possible (young Edward used his position as stenographer to Jay Gould to glean tips on the market,
thereby cleaning up for himself and his Sunday-
school teacher at Plymouth Church), and third,
keeping your eye open for the main chance.

In conclusion, nothing more fitting could be quoted
than the touching caption under the picture of the
author's grandmother, " who counselled each of her
children to make the world a better and more beautiful place to live in — a counsel which is now being
carried on by her grandchildren, one of whom is Edward Bok."

Could detachment of author and hero be more
complete?

XLIII

ZANE GREY'S MOVIE

THE hum of the moving-picture machine is the predominating note in " The Mysterious Rider," Zane Grey's latest contribution to the literature of unrealism. All that is necessary for a complete illusion is the insertion of three or four news photographs at the end, showing how they catch salmon in the Columbia River, the allegorical floats in the Los Angeles Carnival of Roses and the ice-covered fire ruins in the business section of Worcester, Mass.

In order that the change from book to film may be made as quickly as possible, the author has written his story in the language of the moving-picture subtitle. All that the continuity-writer in the studio will have to do will be to take every third sentence from the book and make a subtitle from it. We might save him the trouble and do it here, together with some suggestions for incidental decorations.

Remember, nothing will be quoted below which is not in the exact wording of Zane Grey's text.

LOVE CONQUERS ALL

We first see Columbine Belllounds, adopted daughter of old Belllounds the rancher of Colorado. She is riding along the trail overlooking the valley.

" TODAY GIRLISH ORDEALS AND GRIEFS SEEMED BACK IN THE PAST: SHE WAS A WOMAN AT NINETEEN AND FACE TO FACE WITH THE FIRST GREAT PROBLEM IN HER LIFE." (Suggestion for title decoration: A pair of reluctant feet standing at the junction of a brook and a river.)

She stops to pick some columbines and soliloquizes. The author says: " She spoke aloud, as if the sound of her voice might convince her," but it is not clear from the text just what she expected to be convinced of. Here is her argument to herself:

" COLUMBINE! . . . SO THEY NAMED ME — THOSE MINERS WHO FOUND ME — A BABY — LOST IN THE WOODS — ASLEEP AMONG THE COLUMBINES." (Decorative nasturtiums.)

Having convinced herself in these reassuring words as she stands alone on the ridge in God's great outdoors, she explains that she has promised to marry Jack Belllounds, the worthless son of her foster-father, although any one can tell that she is in love with Wilson Moore, a cow-puncher on the ranch. You will understand what a sacrifice this was to be when the author says that " the lower part of Jack Belllounds's face was weak."

To the ranch comes " Hell-Bent " Wade, the mysterious man of the plains. He applies for a job, and not only that, but he gets it, which gives him a chance to let us know that:

" EIGHTEEN YEARS AGO HE HAD DRIVEN THE WOMAN HE LOVED AWAY FROM HIM, OUT INTO THE WORLD WITH HER BABY GIRL . . . JEALOUS FOOL! . . . TOO LATE HAD HE DISCOVERED HIS FATAL BLUNDER. . . . THAT WAS BENT WADE'S SECRET." (Fancy sketch of a secret.)

And as we already know that Columbine is almost nineteen (I think she told herself this fact aloud once when she was out riding alone, just to convince herself), the shock is not so great as it might have been to hear Wade murmur aloud (doubtless to convince himself too), " Baby would have been — let's see — 'most nineteen years old now — if she'd lived."

Any bets on who Columbine really is?

Let us digress from the scenario a minute to cite a scintillating passage, one of many in the book. Wade is speaking:

" ' You can never tell what a dog is until you

know him. Dogs are like men. Some of 'em look good, but they're really bad. An' that works the other way round.' "

Oscar Wilde stuff, that is. How often have you felt the truth of what Mr. Grey says here, and yet have never been able to put it into words! It is this ability to put thoughts into words that makes him one of our most popular authors today.

But enough of this. " Hell-Bent " Wade determines that his little gel shall not know him as her father, and, furthermore, that she shall not marry Jack Belllounds. So he goes to the cabin of Wils Moore and tells him that Columbine is unhappy at the thought of her approaching — you guessed it — nuptials.

" PARD! SHE LOVES ME — STILL? "

" WILS, HERS IS THE KIND THAT GROWS STRONGER WITH TIME, I KNOW." (Heart and an hour-glass intertwined.)

Let it be said right here, however, that Jack Belllounds, rough and villainous as he is, is the kind of cow-puncher who says to his father: " I still love you, dad, despite the cruel thing you did to me." No cow-puncher who says " despite " can be entirely bad. Neither can he be a cow-puncher.

ZANE GREY'S MOVIE

It is later, after a thrilling series of physical encounters, that Columbine tells Jack Belllounds in so many words that she loves Wils Moore. " Then Wade saw the glory of her — saw her mother again in that proud, fierce uplift of face that flamed red and then blazed white — saw hate and passion and love in all their primal nakedness.

" LOVE HIM! LOVE WILSON MOORE? YES, YOU FOOL! I LOVE HIM! YES! YES! YES! " (Decorative heart, in which a little door slowly opens, showing the face of Columbine.)

But time is short and there is a Semon comedy to follow immediately after this. So all that we can divulge is that Jack has Wils Moore wrongly accused of cattle-rustling, bringing down on his own head the following chatty bit from his affianced bride:

" SO THAT'S YOUR REVENGE. . . . BUT YOU'RE TO RECKON WITH ME, JACK BELLLOUNDS! YOU VILLAIN! YOU DEVIL! YOU "——

It would be unfair to the millions of readers who will struggle for possession of the circulating-library copies of " The Mysterious Rider " to tell just what happens after this. But need we hesitate to divulge that the final subtitle will be:

LOVE CONQUERS ALL

"'I HAVE FAITH AND HOPE AND LOVE, FOR I AM HIS DAUGHTER.' A FAINT, COOL BREEZE STRAYED THROUGH THE ASPENS, RUSTLING THE LEAVES WHISPERINGLY, AND THE SLENDER COLUMBINES, GLEAMING PALE IN THE TWILIGHT LIFTED THEIR SWEET FACES." (Decorative bull.)

XLIV

SUPPRESSING "JURGEN"

O F course it was silly to suppress "Jurgen."
That goes without saying. But it seems
equally silly, because of its being suppressed, to
hail it as high art. It is simply Mr. James Branch
Cabell's quaint way of telling a raw story and it
isn't particularly his own way, either. Personally,
I like the modern method much better.

"Jurgen" is a frank imitation of the old-time
pornographers and although it is a very good imitation, it need not rank Mr. Cabell any higher than
the maker of a plaster-of-paris copy of some Bœotian
sculptural oddity.

The author, in defense of his fortunate book,
lifts his eyebrows and says, "Honi soit." He
claims, and quite rightly, that everything he has
written has at least one decent meaning, and that
anyone who reads anything indecent into it automat-
ically convicts himself of being in a pathological
condition. The question is, if Mr. Cabell had been
convinced beforehand that nowhere in all this broad
land would there be anyone who would read another

meaning into his lily-white words, would he ever have bothered to write the book at all?

Mr. Cabell is admittedly a genealogist. He is an earnest student of the literature of past centuries. He has become so steeped in the phrases and literary mannerisms of the middle and upper-middle ages that, even in his book of modern essays "Beyond Life," he is constantly emitting strange words which were last used by the correspondents who covered the crusades. No man has to be as artificially obsolete as Mr. Cabell is. He likes to be.

In " Jurgen " he has simply let himself go. There is no pretense of writing like a modern. There is no pretense of writing in the style of even James Branch Cabell. It is frankly " in the manner of " those ancient authors whose works are sold surreptitiously to college students by gentlemen who whisper their selling-talk behind a line of red sample bindings. And it is not in the manner of Rabelais, although Rabelais's name has been frequently used in describing " Jurgen." Rabelais seldom hid his thought behind two meanings. There was only one meaning, and you could take it or leave it. And Rabelais would never have said " Honi soit " by way of defense.

The general effect is one of Fielding or Sterne

telling the story of Sir Gawain and the Green
Knight, with their own embellishments, to the boys
at the club.

If all that is necessary to produce a work of art
is to take a drummer's story and tell it in dusty
English, we might try our luck with the modern
smoking-car yarn about the traveling-man who
came to the country hotel late at night, and see
how far we can get with it in the manner of James
Branch Cabell imitating Fielding imitating someone else.

It is a tale which they narrate in Nouveau Ro-
chelle, saying: In the old days there came one night
a traveling man to an inn, and the night was late,
and he was sore beset, what with rag-tag-and-bob-
tail. Eftsoons he made known his wants to the
churl behind the desk, who was named Gogyrvan.
And thus he spake:
"Any rooms?"
"Indeed, sir, no," was Gogyrvan's glose.
"Now but this is an deplorable thing, God wot,"
says the traveling man. "Fie, brother, but you
think awry. Come, don smart your thinking-cap
and answer me again. An' you have forgot my
query; it was: 'Any rooms, bo?'"

Whereat the churl behind the desk gat him down from his stool and closed one eye in a wink.

" There is one room," he says, and places his forefinger along the side of his nose, in the manner of a man who places his forefinger along the side of his nose.

But at this point I am stopped short by the warning passage through the room of a cold, damp current of air as from the grave, and I know that it is one of Mr. Sumner's vice deputies flitting by on his rounds in defense of the public morals. So I can go no further, for public morals must be defended even at the cost of public morality (a statement which means nothing but which sounds rather well, I think. I shall try to work it in again some time).

But perhaps enough has been said to show that it is perfectly easy to write something that will sound classic if you can only remember enough old words. When Mr. Cabell has learned the language, he ought to write a good book in modern English. There are lots of people who read it and they speak very highly of it as a means of expression.

But there are certain things that you cannot express in it without sounding crass, which would be a disadvantage in telling a story like " Jurgen."

XLV

ANTI–IBÁÑEZ

WHILE on the subject of books which we read because we think we ought to, and while Vicente Blasco Ibáñez is on the ocean and can't hear what is being said, let's form a secret society.

I will be one of any three to meet behind a barn and admit that I would not give a good gosh darn if a fortune-teller were to tell me tomorrow that I should never, never have a chance to read another book by the great Spanish novelist.

Any of the American reading public who desire to join this secret society may do so without fear of publicity, as the names will not be given out. The only means of distinguishing a fellow-member will be a tiny gold emblem, to be worn in the lapel, representing the figure (couchant) of Spain's most touted animal. The motto will be " Nimmermehr," which is a German translation of the Spanish phrase " Not even once again."

Simply because I myself am not impressed by a book, I have no authority to brand anyone who does not like it as a poseur and say that he is only making believe that he likes it. And there must be a great many highly literary people who really and sincerely do think that Señor Blasco's books are the finest novels of the epoch.

It would therefore be presumptuous of me to say that Spain is now, for the first time since before 1898, in a position to kid the United States and, vicariously through watching her famous son count his royalties and gate receipts, to feel avenged for the loss of her islands. If America has found something superfine in Ibáñez that his countrymen have missed, then America is of course to be congratulated and not kidded.

But probably no one was more surprised than Blasco when he suddenly found himself a lion in our literary arena instead of in his accustomed rôle of bull in his home ring. And those who know say that you could have knocked his compatriots over with a feather when the news came that old man Ibáñez's son had made good in the United States to the extent of something like five hundred million pesetas.

For, like the prophet whom some one was telling about, Ibáñez was not known at home as a particularly hot tamale. But, then, he never had such a persistent publisher in Spain, and book-advertising is not the art there that it is in America. When the final accounting of the great success of " The Four Horsemen of the Apocalypse " in this country is taken, honorable mention must be made of the man at the E. P. Dutton & Co. store who had charge of the advertising.

The great Spanish novelist was in the French propaganda service during the war. It was his job to make Germany unpopular in Spanish. " The Four Horsemen of the Apocalypse " is obviously propaganda, and not particularly subtle propaganda either. Certain chapters might have come direct from our own Creel committee, and one may still be true to the Allied cause and yet maintain that propaganda and literature do not mix with any degree of illusion.

There is no question, of course, that those chapters in the book which are descriptive of the advance and subsequent retreat of the German troops under the eye of Don Marcelo are masterpieces of descriptive reporting. But Philip Gibbs has given us a whole book of masterpieces of descriptive reporting which do not bear the stamp of approval of the official propaganda bureau. And, furthermore, Philip Gibbs does not wear a sport shirt open at the neck. At least, he never had his picture taken that way.

LOVE CONQUERS ALL

As for the rest of the books that were dragged
out from the Spanish for " storehouse " when " The
Four Horsemen " romped in winners, I can speak
only as I would speak of " The World's Most Famous Battles " or " Heroines in Shakespeare." I
have looked them over. I gave " Mare Nostrum "
a great deal of my very valuable time because the
advertisements spoke so highly of it. " Woman
Triumphant " took less time because I decided to
stop earlier in the book. " Blood and Sand " I
passed up, having once seen a Madrid bull-fight for
myself, which may account for this nasty attitude
I have toward any Spanish product. I am told,
however, that this is the best of them all.

It is remarkable that for a writer who seems to
have left such an indelible imprint in the minds of
the American people, whose works have been ranked
with the greatest of all time and who received more
publicity during one day of his visit here than
Charles Dickens received during his whole sojourn
in America, Señor Blasco and his works form a
remarkably small part of the spontaneous literary
conversation of the day. The characters which he
has created have not taken any appreciable hold
in the public imagination. Their names are never
used as examples of anything. Who were some of
his chief characters, by the way? What did they

say that was worth remembering? What did they do that characters have not been doing for many generations? Did you ever hear anyone say, " He talks like a character in Ibáñez," or " This might have happened in one of Ibáñez's books "?

Of course it is possible for a man to write a great book from which no one would quote. That is probably happening all the time. But it is because no one has read it. Here we have an author whose vogue in this country, according to statistics, is equal to that of any writer of novels in the world. And as soon as his publicity department stops functioning, I should like to lay a little bet that he will not be heard of again.

XLVI

ON BRICKLAYING

AFTER a series of introspective accounts of the babyhood, childhood, adolescence and inevitably gloomy maturity of countless men and women, it is refreshing to turn to " Bricklaying in Modern Practice," by Stewart Scrimshaw. " Heigh-ho! " one says. " Back to normal again! "

For bricklaying is nothing if not normal, and Mr. Scrimshaw has given just enough of the romantic charm of artistic enthusiasm to make it positively fascinating.

" There was a time when man did not know how to lay bricks," he says in his scholarly introductory chapter on " The Ancient Art," " a time when he did not know how to make bricks. There was a time when fortresses and cathedrals were unknown, and churches and residences were not to be seen on the face of the earth. But today we see wonderful architecture, noble and glorious structures, magnificent skyscrapers and pretty home-like bungalows."

To one who has been scouring Westchester

County for the past two months looking at the structures which are being offered for sale as homes, " pretty home-like bungalows " comes as *le mot juste*. They certainly are no more than, pretty home-like.

One cannot read far in Mr. Scrimshaw's book without blushing for the inadequacy of modern education. We are turned out of our schools as educated young men and women, and yet what college graduate here tonight can tell me when the first brick in Amercia was made? Or even where it was made? . . . I thought not.

Well, it was made in New Haven in 1650. Mr. Scrimshaw does not say what it was made for, but a conjecture would be that it was the handiwork of Yale students for tactical use in the Harvard game. (Oh, I know that Yale wasn't running in 1650, but what difference does that make in an informal little article like this? It is getting so that a man can't make any statement at all without being caught up on it by some busybody or other.)

But let's get down to the art itself.

Mr. Scrimshaw's first bit of advice is very sound. " The bricklayer should first take a keen glance at the scaffolding upon which he is to work, to see that there is nothing broken or dangerous connected with it. . . . This is essential, because more important than anything else to him is the preservation of his life and limb."

Oh, Mr. Scrimshaw, how true that is! If I were a bricklayer I would devote practically my whole morning inspecting the scaffolding on which I was to work. Whatever else I shirked, I would put my whole heart and soul into this part of my task. Every rope should be tested, every board examined, and I doubt if even then I would go up on the scaffold. Any bricks that I could not lay with my feet on terra firma (there is a joke somewhere about terra cotta, but I'm busy now) could be laid by some one else.

But we don't seem to be getting ahead in our instruction in practical bricklaying. Well, all right, take this:

"Pressed bricks, which are buttered, can be laid with a one-eighth-inch joint, although a joint of three-sixteenths of an inch is to be preferred."

Joe, get this gentleman a joint of three-sixteenths of an inch, buttered. Service, that's our motto!

It takes a book like this to make a man realize what he misses in his everyday life. For instance, who would think that right here in New York there were people who specialized in corbeling? Rain or shine, hot or cold, you will find them corbeling around like Trojans. Or when they are not corbeling they may be toothing. (I too thought that this might be a misprint for " teething," but it is spelled " toothing " throughout the book, so I guess that Mr. Scrimshaw knows what he is about.) Of all departments of bricklaying I should think that it would be more fun to tooth than to do anything else. But it must be tiring work. I suppose that many a bricklayer's wife has said to her neighbor, " I am having a terrible time with my husband this week. He is toothing, and comes home so cross and irritable that nothing suits him."

Another thing that a bricklayer has to be careful of, according to the author (and I have no reason to contest his warning), is the danger of stepping on spawls. If there is one word that I would leave with the young bricklayer about to enter his trade it is " Beware of the spawls, my boy." They are insidious, those spawls are. You think you are all right and then — pouf! Or maybe " crash " would be a better descriptive word. Whatever noise is made by a spawl when stepped on is the one I want. Perhaps " swawk " would do. I'll have to look up " spawl " first, I guess.

LOVE CONQUERS ALL

Well, anyway, there you have practical brick-laying in a nutshell. Of course there are lots of other points in the book and some dandy pictures and it would pay you to read it. But in case you haven't time, just skim over this résumé again and you will have the gist of it.

XLVII

"AMERICAN ANNIVERSARIES"

MR. PHILIP R. DILLON has compiled and published in his "American Anniversaries" a book for men who do things. For every day in the year there is a record of something which has been accomplished in American history. For instance, under Jan. 1 we find that the parcel-post system was inaugurated in the United States in 1913, while Jan. 2 is given as the anniversary of the battle of Murfreesboro (or Stone's River, as you prefer). The whole book is like that; just one surprise after another.

What, for instance, do you suppose that Saturday marked the completion of? . . . Presuming that no one has answered correctly, I will disclose (after consulting Mr. Dillon's book) that July 31 marked the completion of the 253d year since the signing of the Treaty of Breda. But what, you may say — and doubtless are saying at this very minute — what has the Treaty of Breda (which everyone knows was signed in Holland by representatives of England, France, Holland and Denmark) got to do with

American history? And right there is where Mr. Dillon and I would have you. In the Treaty of Breda, Acadia (or Nova Scotia) was given to France and New York and New Jersey were confirmed to England. So, you see, inhabitants of New York and New Jersey (and, after all, who isn't?) should have especial cause for celebrating July 31 as Breda Day, for if it hadn't been for that treaty we might have belonged to Poland and been mixed up in all the mess that is now going on over there.

I must confess that I turned to the date of the anniversary of my own birth with no little expectation. Of course I am not so very well known except among the tradespeople in my town, but I should be willing to enter myself in a popularity contest with the Treaty of Breda. But evidently there is a conspiracy of silence directed against me on the part of the makers of anniversary books and calendars. While no mention was made of my having been born on Sept. 15, considerable space was given to recording the fact that on that date in 1840 a patent for a knitting machine was issued to the inventor, who was none other than Isaac Wixan Lamb of Salem, Mass.

Now I would be the last one to belittle the importance of knitting or the invention of a knitting machine. I know some very nice people who knit a great deal. But really, when it comes to anniversaries I don't see where Isaac Wixon Lamb gets off to crash in ahead of me or a great many other people that I could name. And it doesn't help any, either, to find that James Fenimore Cooper and William Howard Taft are both mentioned as having been born on that day or that the chief basic patent for gasoline automobiles in America was issued in 1895 to George B. Selden. It certainly was a big day for patents. But one realizes more than ever after reading this section that you have to have a big name to get into an anniversary book. The average citizen has no show at all.

In spite of these rather obvious omissions, Mr. Dillon's book is both valuable and readable. Especially in those events which occurred early in the country's history is there material for comparison with the happenings of the present day, events which will some day be incorporated in a similar book compiled by some energetic successor of Mr. Dillon.

For instance, under Oct. 27, 1659, we find that William Robinson and Marmaduke Stevenson were banished from New Hampshire on the charge of being Quakers and were later executed for returning to the colony. Imagine!

And on Dec. 8, 1837, Wendell Phillips delivered his first abolition speech at Boston in Faneuil Hall, as a result of which he got himself known around Boston as an undesirable citizen, a dangerous radical and a revolutionary trouble-maker. It hardly seems possible now, does it?

And on July 4, 1776 — but there, why rub it in?

XLVIII

A WEEK-END WITH WELLS

IN the February Bookman there is an informal article by John Elliot called " At Home with H. G. Wells " in which we are let in on the ground floor in the Wells household and shown " H. G." (as his friends and his wife call him) at play. It is an interesting glimpse at the small doings of a great man, but there is one feature of those doings which has an ominous sound.

" The Wells that everyone loves who sees him at Easton is the human Wells, the family Wells, the jovial Wells, Wells the host of some Sunday afternoon party. For a distance of ten or twenty miles round folks come on Sunday to play hockey and have tea. Old and young — people from down London who never played hockey before in their lives; country farmers and their daughters, and everybody else who lives in the district — troop over and bring whoever happens to be the week-end guest. Wells is delightful to them all. He doesn't give a rap if they are solid Tories, Bolsheviks, Liberals, or men and women of no political leanings,

Can you play hockey? is all that matters. If you say No you are rushed toward a pile of sticks and given one and told to go in the forward line; if you say Yes you are probably made a vice captain on the spot."

I am frank to confess that this sounds perfectly terrible to me. I can't imagine a worse place in which to spend a week-end than one where your host is always boisterously forcing you to take part in games and dances about which you know nothing. A week-end guest ought to be ignored, allowed to rummage about alone among the books, live stock and cold food in the ice-box whenever he feels like it, and not rushed willy-nilly (something good could be done using the famous Willy-Nilly correspondence as a base, but not here), into whatever the family itself may consider a good time.

In such a household as the Wells household must be you are greeted by your hostess in a robust manner with " So glad you're on time. The match begins at two." And when you say " What match, " you are told that there is a little tennis tournament on for the week-end and that you and Hank are scheduled to start the thing off with a bang. " But I haven't played tennis for five years," you protest, thinking of the delightful privacy of your own little hall bedroom in town. " Never mind, it will all come back to you. Bill has got some extra things all put out for you upstairs." So you start off your week-end by making a dub of yourself and are known from that afternoon on by the people who didn't catch your name as " the man who had such a funny serve."

Or if it isn't that, it's dancing. Immediately after dinner, just as you are about to settle down for a comfortable evening by the fire, you notice that they are rolling back the rugs. " House-cleaning? " you suggest, with a nervous little laugh. " Oh, no, just a little dancing in your honor." And then you tell them that your honor will be satisfied perfectly without dancing, that you haven't danced since you left school, that you don't dance very well, or that you have hurt your foot; to which the only reply is an encouraging laugh and a hail-fellow-well-met push out into the middle of the floor.

A pox on both your house parties!

And yet, in a way, that is just what one might expect from Mr. Wells. He has done the same thing to me in his books many a time. I personally have but little facility for world-repairing. I haven't the slightest idea of how one would go about making things better. And yet before I am more than two-

thirds of the way through " Joan and Peter " or
" The Undying Fire " or " The Outline of History,"
Mr. Wells has me out on the hockey-field waving
a stick with a magnificent enthusiasm but no aim,
rushing up and down and calling, " Come on, now! "
to no one in particular.

No matter how discouraging things seem when I
pick up a Wells book, or how averse I may be to
launching out on a crusade of any sort, I always
end by walking with a firm step to the door (feeling,
somehow, that I have grown quite a bit taller and
much handsomer) and saying quietly: " Meadows,
my suit of armor, please; the one with a chain-mail
shirt and a purple plume."

This, of course, is silly, as any of Mr. Wells's
critics will tell you. It is the effect that he has on
irresponsible, visionary minds. But if all the irresponsible, visionary minds in the world become sufficiently belligerent through a continued reading of
Mr. Wells, or even of the New Testament, who
knows but what they may become just practical
enough to take a hand at running things? They
couldn't do much worse than the responsible, practical minds have done, now, could they?

XLIX

ABOUT PORTLAND CEMENT

PORTLAND cement is " the finely pulverized product resulting from the calcination to incipient fusion of an intimate mixture of properly proportioned argillaceous and calcareous materials and to which no addition greater than 3 per cent has been made subsequent to calcination."

That, in a word, is the keynote of H. Colin Campbell's " How to Use Cement for Concrete Construction." In case you should never read any more of the book, you would have that.

But to the reader who is not satisfied with this taste of the secret of cement construction and who reads on into Mr. Campbell's work, there is revealed a veritable mine of information. And in the light of the recent turn of events one might even call it significant. (Any turn of events will do.)

The first chapter is given over to a plea for concrete. Judging from the claims made for concrete by Mr. Campbell, it will accomplish everything that a return to Republican administration would do, and wouldn't be anywhere near so costly. It will make your barn fireproof; it will insure clean milk for your children; it will provide a safe housing for your automobile. Farm prosperity and concrete go hand in hand.

In case there are any other members of society who have been with me in thinking that Portland cement is a product of Portland, Me., or Portland, Ore., it might as well be stated right here and now that America had nothing to do with the founding of the industry, and that the lucky Portland is an island off the south coast of England.

It was a bright sunny afternoon in May, 1824, when Joseph Aspdin, an intelligent bricklayer of Leeds, England, was carelessly calcining a mixture of limestone and clay, as bricklayers often do on their days off, that he suddenly discovered, on reducing the resulting clinker to a powder, that this substance, on hardening, resembled nothing so much as the yellowish-gray stone found in the quarries on the Isle of Portland. (How Joe knew what grew on the Isle of Portland when his home was in Leeds is not explained. Maybe he spent his summers at the Portland House, within three minutes of the bathing beach.)

At any rate, on discovering the remarkable similarity between the mess he had cooked up and Portland stone, he called to his wife and said: "Eunice, come here a minute! What does this remind you of? "

The usually cheerful brow of Eunice Aspdin clouded for the fraction of a second.

" That night up at Bert and Edna's? " she ventured.

" No, no, my dear," said the intelligent bricklayer, slightly irked. " Anyone could see that this here substance is a dead ringer for Portland stone, and I am going to make heaps and heaps of it and call it ' Portland cement.' It is little enough that I can do for the old island."

And so that's how Portland cement was named. Rumor hath it that the first Portland cement in America was made at Allentown, Pa., in 1875, but I wouldn't want to be quoted as having said that. But I will say that the total annual production in this country is now over 90,000,000 barrels.

It is interesting to note that cement is usually packed in cloth sacks, although sometimes paper bags are used.

" A charge is made for packing cement in paper bags," the books says. " These, of course, are not redeemable."

One can understand their not wanting to take

back a paper bag in which cement has been wrapped. The wonder is that the bag lasts until you get home with it. I tried to take six cantaloups home in a paper bag the other night and had a bad enough time of it. Cement, when it is in good form, must be much worse than cantaloup, and the redeemable remnants of the bag must be negligible. But why charge extra for using paper bags? That seems like adding whatever it is you add to injury. Apologies, rather than extra charge, should be in order. However, I suppose that these cement people understand their business. I shall know enough to watch out, however, and insist on having whatever cement I may be called upon to carry home done up in a cloth sack. "Not in a paper bag, if you please," I shall say very politely to the clerk.

L

OPEN BOOKCASES

THINGS have come to a pretty pass when a man can't buy a bookcase that hasn't got glass doors on it. What are we becoming — a nation of weaklings?

All over New York city I have been, — trying to get something in which to keep books. And what am I shown? Curio cabinets, inclosed whatnots, museum cases in which to display fragments from the neolithic age, and glass-faced sarcophagi for dead butterflies.

"But I am apt to use my books at any time," I explain to the salesman. "I never can tell when it is coming on me. And when I want a book I want it quickly. I don't want to have to send down to the office for the key, and I don't want to have to manipulate any trick ball-bearings and open up a case as if I were getting cream-puffs out for a customer. I want a bookcase for books and not books for a bookcase."

(I really don't say all those clever things to the clerk. It took me quite a while to think them up.

What I really say is, timidly, " Haven't you any bookcases without glass doors? " and when they say " No," I thank them and walk into the nearest dining-room table.)

But if they keep on getting arrogant about it I shall speak up to them one of these fine days. When I ask for an open-faced bookcase they look with a scornful smile across the salesroom toward the mahogany four-posters and say:

" Oh, no, we don't carry those any more. We don't have any call for them. Every one uses the glass-doored ones now. They keep the books much cleaner."

Then the ideal procedure for a real book-lover would be to keep his books in the original box, snugly packed in excelsior, with the lid nailed down. Then they would be nice and clean. And the sun couldn't get at them and ruin the bindings. Faugh! (Try saying that. It doesn't work out at all as you think it's going to. And it makes you feel very silly for having tried it.)

Why, in the elder days bookcases with glass doors were owned only by people who filled them with ten volumes of a pictorial history of the Civil War (including some swell steel engravings), " Walks

I thank them and walk into the nearest dining-room table.

and Talks with John L. Stoddard " and " Daily Thoughts for Daily Needs," done in robin's-egg blue with a watered silk bookmark dangling out. A set of Sir Walter Scott always helps fill out a bookcase with glass doors. It looks well from the front and shows that you know good literature when you see it. And you don't have to keep opening and shutting the doors to get it out, for you never want to get it out.

A bookcase with glass doors used to be a sign that somewhere in the room there was a crayon portrait of Father when he was a young man, with a real piece of glass stuck on the portrait to represent a diamond stud.

And now we are told that " every one buys bookcases with glass doors; we have no call for others." Soon we shall be told that the thing to do is to buy the false backs of bindings, such as they have in stage libraries, to string across behind the glass. It will keep us from reading too much, and then, too, no one will want to borrow our books.

But one clerk told me the truth. And I am just fearless enough to tell it here. I know that it will kill my chances for the Presidency, but I cannot stop to think of that.

After advising me to have a carpenter build me

the kind of bookcase I wanted, and after I had told him that I had my name in for a carpenter but wasn't due to get him until late in the fall, as he was waiting for prices to go higher before taking the job on, the clerk said:

" That's it. It's the price. You see the furniture manufacturers can make much more money out of a bookcase with glass doors than they can without. When by hanging glass doors on a piece of furniture at but little more expense to themselves they can get a much bigger profit, what's the sense in making them without glass doors? They have just stopped making them, that's all."

So you see the American people are being practically forced into buying glass doors whether they want them or not. Is that right? Is it fair? Where is our personal liberty going to? What is becoming of our traditional American institutions?

I don't know.

LI

TROUT–FISHING

I NEVER knew very much about trout-fishing anyway, and I certainly had no inkling that a trout-fisher had to be so deceitful until I read "Trout-Fishing in Brooks," by G. Garrow-Green. The thing is appalling. Evidently the sport is nothing but a constant series of compromises with one's better nature, what with sneaking about pretending to be something that one is not, trying to fool the fish into thinking one thing when just the reverse is true, and in general behaving in an underhanded and tricky manner throughout the day.

The very first and evidently the most important exhortation in the book is, "Whatever you do, keep out of sight of the fish." Is that open and above-board? Is it honorable?

"Trout invariably lie in running water with their noses pointed against the current, and therefore whatever general chance of concealment there may be rests in fishing from behind them. The moral is that the brook-angler must both walk and fish upstream."

LOVE CONQUERS ALL

It seems as if a lot of trouble might be saved the fisherman, in case he really didn't want to walk upstream but had to get to some point downstream before 6 o'clock, to adopt some disguise which would deceive the fish into thinking that he had no intention of catching them anyway. A pair of blue glasses and a cane would give the effect of the wearer being blind and harmless, and could be thrown aside very quickly when the time came to show one's self in one's true colors to the fish. If there were two anglers they might talk in loud tones about their dislike for fish in any form, and then, when the trout were quite reassured and swimming close to the bank they could suddenly be shot with a pistol.

But a little further on comes a suggestion for a much more elaborate bit of subterfuge.

The author says that in the early season trout are often engaged with larvæ at the bottom and do not show on the surface. It is then a good plan, he says, to sink the flies well, moving in short jerks to imitate nymphs.

You can see that imitating a nymph will call for a lot of rehearsing, but I doubt very much if moving in short jerks is the way in which to go about it. I have never actually seen a nymph, though if I had I should not be likely to admit it, and I can think of no possible way in which I could give an adequate illusion of being one myself. Even the most stupid of trout could easily divine that I was masquerading, and then the question would immediately arise in its mind: "If he is not a nymph, then what is his object in going about like that trying to imitate one? He is up to no good, I'll be bound."

And crash! away would go the trout before I could put my clothes back on.

There is an interesting note on the care and feeding of worms on page 67. One hundred and fifty worms are placed in a tin and allowed to work their way down into packed moss.

"A little fresh milk poured in occasionally is sufficient food," writes Mr. Garrow-Green, in the style of Dr. Holt. "So disposed, the worms soon become bright, lively and tough."

It is easy to understand why one should want to have bright worms, so long as they don't know that they are bright and try to show off before company, but why deliberately set out to make them tough? Good manners they may not be expected to acquire, but a worm with a cultivated vulgarity sounds intolerable. Imagine 150 very

tough worms all crowded together in one tin!
" Canaille " is the only word to describe it.

I suppose that it is my ignorance of fishing par-
lance which makes the following sentence a bit
hazy:

" Much has been written about bringing a fish
downstream to help drown it, as no doubt it does;
still, this is often impracticable."

I can think of nothing more impracticable than
trying to drown a fish under any conditions,
upstream or down, but I suppose that Mr. Garrow-Green knows what he is talking about.

And in at least one of his passages I follow him
perfectly. In speaking of the time of day for fly-
fishing in the spring he says:

" ' Carpe diem ' is a good watchword when trout
are in the humor." At least, I know a good pun
when I see one.

LII

"SCOUTING FOR GIRLS"

" SCOUTING for Girls " is not the kind of book you think it is. The verb " to scout " is intransitive in this case. As a matter of fact, instead of being a volume of advice to men on how to get along with girls, it is full of advice to girls on how to get along without men, that is, within reason, of course.

It is issued by the Girl Scouts and is very subtle anti-man propaganda. I can't find that men are mentioned anywhere in the book. It is given over entirely to telling girls how to chop down trees, tie knots in ropes, and things like that. Now, as a man, I am very jealous of my man's prerogative of chopping down trees and tying knots in ropes, and I resent the teaching of young girls to usurp my province in these matters. Any young girl who has taken one lesson in knot-tying will be able to make me appear very silly at it. After two lessons she could tie me hand and foot to a tree and go away with my watch and commutation ticket. And then I would look fine, wouldn't I? Small wonder to me that I hail the Girl Scout movement as a menace and urge its being nipped in the bud as you would nip a viper in the bud. I would not be surprised if there were Russian Soviet money back of it somewhere.

A companion volume to " Scouting for Girls " is " Campward, Ho! " a manual for Girl Scout camps. The keynote is sounded on the first page by a quotation from Chaucer, beginning:

> *" When that Aprille with his schowres*
> *swoote*
> *The drought of March hath perced to the*
> *roote,*
> *And bathus every veyne in swich licour,*
> *Of which vertue engendred is the flour."*

One can almost hear the girls singing that of an evening as they sit around the camp-fire tying knots in ropes. It is really an ideal camping song, because even the littlest girls can sing the words without understanding what they mean.

But it really lacks the lilt of the " Marching Song " printed further on in the book. This is to be sung to the tune of " Where Do We Go From Here, Boys? " Bear this in mind while humming it to yourself:

" SCOUTING FOR GIRLS "

MARCHING SONG

Where do we go from here, girls, where do
*   we go from here?*
Anywhere (our Captain*) leads we'll
*   follow, never fear.*
The world is full of dandy girls, but wait
*   till we appear —*
*   Then!*
Girl Scouts, Girl Scouts, give us a hearty
*   cheer!*

* Supply Captain's name.

A very stirring marching song, without doubt,
but what would they do if the leader's name
happened to be something like Mary Louise Aber-
crombie or Elizabeth Van Der Water? They just
couldn't have a Captain with such a long name,
that's all. And there you have unfair discrimina-
tion creeping into your camp right at the start.

In " Scouting for Girls " there is some useful
information concerning smoke signals. In case you
are lost, or want to communicate with your friends
who are beyond shouting distance, it is much
quicker than telephoning to build a clear, hot fire
and cover it with green stuff or rotten wood so that

it will send up a solid column of black smoke. **By** spreading and lifting a blanket over this smudge the column can be cut up into pieces, long or short (this is the way it explains it in the book, but it doesn't sound plausible to me), and by a preconcerted code these can be made to convey tidings.

For instance, one steady smoke means " Here is camp."

Two steady smokes mean " I am lost. Come and help me."

Three smokes in a row mean " Good news! "

I suppose that the Pollyanna of the camping party is constantly sending up three smokes in a row on the slightest provocation, and then when the rest of the outfit have raced across country for miles to find out what the good news is she probably shows them, with great enthusiasm, that some fringed gentians are already in blossom or that the flicker's eggs have hatched. Unfortunately, there is no smoke code given for snappy replies, but in the next paragraph it tells how to carry on a conversation with pistol shots. One of these would serve the purpose for repartee.

LIII

HOW TO SELL GOODS

THE Retail Merchants' Association ought to buy up all the copies of " Elements of Retail Salesmanship," by Paul Westley Ivey (Macmillan), and not let a single one get into the hands of a customer, for once the buying public reads what is written there the game is up. It tells all about how to sell goods to people, how to appeal to their weaknesses, how to exert subtle influences which will win them over in spite of themselves. Houdini might as well issue a pamphlet giving in detail his methods of escape as for the merchants of this country to let this book remain in circulation.

The art of salesmanship is founded, according to Mr. Ivey, on, first, a thorough knowledge of the goods which are to be sold, and second, a knowledge of the customer. By knowing the customer you know what line of argument will most appeal to him. There are several lines in popular use. First is the appeal to the instinct of self-preservation — i.e., social self-preservation. The customer is made to feel that in order to preserve her social standing she must buy the article in question. " She must be made to feel what a disparaged social self would mean to her mental comfort."

It is reassuring to know that it is a recognized ruse on the part of the salesman to intimate that unless you buy a particular article you will have to totter through life branded as the arch-piker. I have always taken this attitude of the clerks perfectly seriously. In fact, I have worried quite a bit about it.

In the store where I am allowed to buy my clothes it is quite the thing among the salesmen to see which one of them can degrade me most. They intimate that, while they have no legal means of refusing to sell their goods to me, it really would be much more in keeping with things if I were to take the few pennies that I have at my disposal and run around the corner to some little haberdashery for my shirts and ties. Every time I come out from that store I feel like Ethel Barrymore in " Déclassée." Much worse, in fact, for I haven't any good looks to fall back upon.

But now that I know the clerks are simply acting all that scorn in an attempt to appeal to my instinct for the preservation of my social self, I can face them without flinching. When that pompous

They intimate that I had better take my few pennies and
run 'round the corner to some little haberdashery.

old boy with the sandy mustache who has always looked upon me as a member of the degenerate Juke family tries to tell me that if I don't take the five-dollar cravat he won't be responsible for the way in which decent people will receive me when I go out on the street, I will reach across the counter and playfully pull his own necktie out from his waistcoat and scream, " I know you, you old rascal! You got that stuff from page 68 of ' Elements of Retail Salesmanship ' (Macmillan)."

Other traits which a salesperson may appeal to in the customer are: Vanity, parental pride, greed, imitation, curiosity and selfishness. One really gets in touch with a lot of nice people in this work and can bring out the very best that is in them.

Customers are divided into groups indicative of temperament. There is first the Impulsive or Nervous Customer. She is easily recognized because she walks into the store in " a quick, sometimes jerky manner. Her eyes are keen-looking; her expression is intense, oftentimes appearing strained." She must be approached promptly, according to the book, and what she desires must be quickly ascertained. Since these are the rules for selling to people who enter the store in this manner, it might be well, no matter how lethargic you may be by nature, to assume the appearance of the Impulsive or Nervous Customer as soon as you enter the store, adopting a quick, even jerky manner and making your eyes as keen-looking as possible, with an intense expression, oftentimes appearing strained. Then the clerk will size you up as type No. 1 and will approach you promptly. After she has quickly filled your order you may drop the impulsive pose and assume your natural, slow manner again, whereupon the clerk will doubtless be highly amused at having been so cleverly fooled into giving quick service.

The opposite type is known as the Deliberate Customer. She walks slowly and in a dignified manner. Her facial expression is calm and poised. "Gestures are uncommon, but if existing tend to be slow and inconspicuous." She can wait.

Then there is the Vacillating or Indecisive Customer, the Confident or Decisive Customer (this one should be treated with subtle flattery and agreement with all her views), the Talkative or Friendly Customer, and the Silent or Indifferent one. All these have their little weaknesses, and the perfect salesperson will learn to know these and play to them.

There seems to be only one thing left for the

customer to do in order to meet this concerted attack upon his personality. That is, to hire some expert like Mr. Ivey to study the different types of sales men and women and formulate methods of meeting their offensive. Thus, if I am of the type designated as the Vacillating or Indecisive Customer, I ought to know what to do when confronted by a salesman of the Aristocratic, Scornful type, so that I may not be bulldozed into buying something I do not want.

If I could only find such a book of instructions I would go tomorrow and order a black cotton engineer's shirt from that sandy-mustached salesman and bawl him out if he raised his eyebrows. But not having the book, I shall go in and, without a murmur, buy a $3 silk shirt for $18 and slink out feeling that if I had been any kind of sport at all I would also have bought that cork helmet in the showcase.

LIV

" YOU! "

IN the window of the grocery store to which I
used to be sent after a pound of Mocha and
Java mixed and a dozen of your best oranges, there
was a cardboard figure of a clerk in a white coat
pointing his finger at the passers-by. As I remember, he was accusing you of not taking home
a bottle of Moxie, and pretty guilty it made you
feel too.

This man was, I believe, the pioneer in what has
since become a great literary movement. He
founded the " You, Mr. Business-Man! " school of
direct appeal. It is strictly an advertising property
and has long been used to sell merchandise to people
who never can resist the flattery of being addressed
personally. When used as an advertisement it is
usually accompanied by an illustration built along
the lines of the pioneer grocery-clerk, pointing a
virile finger at you from the page of the magazine,
and putting the whole thing on a personal basis by
addressing you as " You, Mr. Rider-in-the-Open-

" YOU! "

Cars! " or " You, Mr. Wearer-of-14½-Shirts! " The appeal is instantaneous.

In straight reading-matter, bound in book form and sold as literature, this Moxie talk becomes a volume of inspirational sermonizing, and instead of selling cooling drinks or warming applications, it throws dynamic paragraph after dynamic paragraph into the fight for efficiency, concentration, self-confidence and personality on the part of our body politic. A homely virtue such as was taught us at our mother's knee (or across our mother's knees) at the age of four, in a dozen or so simple words, is taken and blown up into a book in which it is stated very impressively in a series of short, snappy sentences, all saying the same thing.

Such a book is called, for instance " You," written by Irving R. Allen.

" You " takes 275 pages to divulge a secret of success. It would not be fair to Mr. Allen to give it away here after he has spent so much time concealing it. But it might be possible to give some idea of the importance of Mr. Allen's discovery by stating one of my own, somewhat in the manner in which he has stated his. I will give my little contribution to the world's inspiration the title of

HEY, YOU!

You and I are alone.

No, don't try to get away. That door is locked. I won't hurt you — much.

What I want to do is make you see yourself. I want you, when you put down this book, to say, " I know myself! " I want you to be able to look at yourself in the mirror and say: " Why, certainly I remember you, Mr. Addington Simms of Seattle, you old Rotary Club dog! How's your merger? "

And the only way that you can ever be able to do this is to read this book through.

Then read it through again.

Then read it through again.

Then ring Dougherty's bell and ask for " Chester."

Now let's get down to business.

I knew a man once who had made a million dollars. If he hadn't been arrested he would have made another million.

Do you see what I mean?

If not, go back and read that over a second time. It's worth it. I wrote it for you to read. You, do you hear me? You!

If you want to know the secret of this man's success, of the success of hundreds of other men just like him, if you want to make his success your success, you must first learn the rule.

What is this rule? you may ask.

Go ahead and ask it.

Very well, since you ask.

It is a rule which has kept J. P. Morgan what he is. It is a rule which gives John D. Rockefeller the right to be known as the Baptist man alive. It is a rule which is responsible for the continued existence of every successful man of today.

And now I am going to tell it to you.

You, the you that you know, the real you, are going to learn the secret.

Can you bear it?

Here it is:

You can't win if you breathe under water.

Read that again.

Read it backward.

It may sound simple to you now. You may say to yourself, " What do you take me for, a baby boy? "

Well, you paid good money for this book, didn't you?

LV

THE CATALOGUE SCHOOL

WITHOUT wishing in the least to detract from the praise due to Sinclair Lewis for the remarkable accuracy with which he reports details in his " Main Street," it is interesting to speculate on how other books might have read had their authors had Mr. Lewis's flair for minutiæ and their publishers enough paper to print the result.

For instance, Carol Kennicott, the heroine, whenever she is overtaken by an emotional scene, is given to looking out at the nearest window to hide her feelings, whereupon the author goes to great lengths to describe just exactly what came within her range of vision. Nothing escapes him, even to shreds of excelsior lying on the ground in back of Howland & Gould's grocery store.

Let us suppose that Harriet Beecher Stowe had been endowed with Mr. Lewis's gift for reporting and had indulged herself in it to the extent of the following in " Uncle Tom's Cabin: "

" Slowly Simon Legree raised his whip-arm to

[274]

strike the prostrate body of the old negro. As he did so his eye wandered across the plantation to the slaves' quarters which crouched blistering in the sun. Cowed as they were, as only ramshackle buildings can be cowed, they presented their gray boards, each eaten with four or five knot-holes, to the elements in abject submission. The door of one hung loose by a rust-encased hinge, of which only one screw remained on duty, and that by sheer willpower of two or three threads. Legree could not quite make out how many threads there were on the screw, but he guessed, and Simon Legree's guess was nearly always right. On the ground at the threshold lay a banjo G string, curled like a blond snake ready to strike at the reddish, brown inner husk of a nut of some sort which was blowing about within reach. There were also several crumbs of corn-pone, well-done, a shred of tobacco which had fallen from the pipe of some negro slave before the fire had consumed more than its very tip, an old shoe which had, Legree noticed by the maker's name, been bought in Boston in its palmier days, doubtless by a Yankee cousin of one of Uncle Tom's former owners, and an indiscriminate pile of old second editions of a Richmond newspaper, sweet-potato peelings and seeds of unripe watermelons.

LOVE CONQUERS ALL

" Swish!   The blow descended on the crouching form of Uncle Tom."

Or Sir Walter Scott:
" Sadly Rowena turned from her lover's side and looked out over the courtyard of the castle. Beneath her she saw the cobble-stones all scratched and marred with gray bruises from the horses' hoofs, a faded purple ribbon dropped from the mandolin of a minstrel, three slightly imperfect wassails and a trencher with a nick on the rim, all that had not been used of the wild boar at last night's feast, a peach-stone like a wrinkled almond nestling in a sardine tin. Slowly she faced her knight:
" ' Prithee,' she said."

And I am not at all sure that " Uncle Tom's Cabin " and " Ivanhoe " wouldn't have made better reading if they had lapsed into the photographic at times.   Mr. Lewis may overdo it, but I expect to re-read " Main Street " some day, and that is more encouragement than I can hold out to Mrs. Stowe or Sir Walter Scott.

LVI

" EFFECTIVE HOUSE ORGANS "

TO the hurrying commuter as he waits for his two cents change at the news stand it looks as if all the periodicals in the United States were on display there, none of which he ever has quite time enough to buy. It seems incredible that there should be presses enough in the country to print all the matter that he sees hanging from wires, piled on the counter and dangling from clips over the edge, to say nothing of his conceiving of there being other periodicals in circulation which he never even hears about. But any one knowing the commuter well enough to call him " dearie " might tell him in slightly worn vernacular that he doesn't know the half of it.

One cannot get a true idea of the amount of side-line printing that is done in this country without reading " Effective House Organs," written by Robert E. Ramsay. The mass effect of this book is appalling. Page after page of clear-cut illustrations show reproductions of hundreds and hundreds of house-organ covers and give the reader a hope-

less sensation of going down for the third time.
Such names as " Gas Logic," " Crane-ing," " Hidden's Hints," " The Y. and E. Idea," " Vim,"
" Tick Talk " and " The Smileage " show that
Yankee ingenuity has invaded the publishing field,
which means that the literature of business is on
its way to becoming the literature of the land.

For those who are so illiterate as not to be familiar with the literature of business, I quote a
definition of the word " house organ ":

" A house magazine or bulletin to dealers, customers or employees, designed to promote goodwill, increase sales, induce better salesmanship or
develop better profits."

In spite of Mr. Ramsay's exceedingly thorough
treatment of his subject, there is one type of house
organ to which he devotes much too little space.
This is the so-called " employee or internal house
organ " and is designed to keep the help happy and
contented with their lot and to spur them on to
extra effort in making it a banner year for the
stockholders. The possibilities of this sort of house
organ in the solution of the problem of industrial
unrest are limitless.

Publications for light reading among employees
are usually called by such titles as " Diblee Do-

ings," " Tinkham Topics," " The Mooney and Car-
miechal Machine Lather " or " Better Belting
News."

First of all, they carry news notes of happenings
among the employees, so that a real spirit of co-
operation and team-play may be fostered. These
news notes include such as the following:

" Eddie Lingard of the Screen Room force, was
observed last Saturday evening between the mystic
hours of six-thirty with a certain party from the
Shipping Room, said party in a tan knit sweater,
on their way to Ollie's. Come, 'fess up, Eddie! "

" Everyone is wondering who the person is who
put chocolate peppermints in some of the girls'
pockets while they were hanging in the Girls' Rest
Room Thursday afternoon, it being so hot that
they melted and practically ruined some of their
clothing. Some folks have a funny sense of
humor."

Then there are excerpts from speeches made by
the Rev. Charles Aubrey Eaton and young Mr.
Rockefeller or by the President and Treasurer of the
Diamond Motor Sales Corporation, saying, in part:

" The man who makes good in any line of work
is the man who gives the best there is in him. He
doesn't watch the clock. He doesn't kick when he

fails to get that raise that he may have expected. He just digs into the job harder and makes the dust fly. And when some one comes along waving a red flag and tries to make him stop work and strike for more money, he turns on the agitator and says: ' You get the h—— out of here. I know my job better than you do. I know my boss better than you do, and I know that he is going to give me the square deal just as soon as he can see his way clear to do it. And in the mean time I am going to WORK! '

" That is the kind of man who makes good."

And then there are efficiency contests, with the force divided into teams trying to see which one can wrap the most containers or stamp the largest number of covers in the week. The winning team gets a felt banner and their names are printed in full in that week's issue of " Pep " or " Nosey News."

And biographies of employees who have been with the company for more than fifty years, with photographs, and a little notice written by the Superintendent saying that this will show the company's appreciation of Mr. Gomble's loyal and unswerving allegiance to his duty, implying that any one else who does his duty for fifty years will also get his picture in the paper and a notice by the Superintendent.

It will easily be seen how this sort of house organ can be made to promote good feeling and esprit de corps among the help. If only more concerns could be prevailed upon to bring this message of weekly or monthly good cheer to their employees, who knows but what the whole caldron of industrial unrest might not suddenly simmer down to mere nothingness? It has been said that all that is necessary is for capital and labor to understand each other. Certainly such a house organ helps the employees to understand their employers.

Perhaps some one will start a house organ edited by the employees for circulation among the bosses, containing newsy notes about the owners' families, quotations from Karl Marx and the results of the profit-sharing contest between the various mills of the district.

This would complete the circle of understanding.

LVII

ADVICE TO WRITERS

TWO books have emerged from the hundreds that are being published on the art of writing. One of them is " The Lure of the Pen," by Flora Klickmann, and the other is " Learning to Write," a collection of Stevenson's meditations on the subject, issued by Scribners. At first glance one might say that the betting would be at least eight to one on Stevenson. But for real, solid, sensible advice in the matter of writing and selling stories in the modern market, Miss Klickmann romps in an easy winner.

It must be admitted that John William Rogers Jr., who collected the Stevenson material, warns the reader in his introduction that the book is not intended to serve as " a macadamized, mile-posted road to the secret of writing," but simply as a help to those who want to write and who are interested to know how Stevenson did it. So we mustn't compare it too closely with Miss Klickmann's book, which is quite frankly a mile-posted road, with little sub-headings along the side of the page such as we used to have in Fiske's Elementary American History. But Miss Klickmann will save the editors of the country a great deal more trouble than Stevenson's advice ever will. She is the editor of an English magazine herself, and has suffered.

Where Miss Klickmann enumerates the pitfalls which the candidate must avoid and points out qualities which every good piece of writing should have, Stevenson writes a delightful essay on " The Profession of Letters " or " A Gossip on Romance." These essays are very inspiring. They are too inspiring. They make the reader feel that he can go out and write like Stevenson. And then a lot of two-cent stamps are wasted and a lot more editors are cross when they get home at night.

On the other hand, the result of Miss Klickmann's book is to make the reader who feels a writing spell coming on stop and give pause. He finds enumerated among the horrors of manuscript-reading several items which he was on the point of injecting into his own manuscript with considerable pride. He may decide that the old job in the shipping-room isn't so bad after all, with its little envelope coming in regularly every week. As a former member of the local manuscript-readers' union, I will give one of three rousing cheers for any good work that Miss Klickmann may do in this field. One writer kept very busy at work in the shipping-room every day is a victory for literature. I used to have a job in a shipping-room myself, so I know.

If, for instance, the subject under discussion were that of learning to skate, Miss Klickmann might advise as follows:

1. Don't try to skate if your ankles are weak.
2. Get skates that fit you. A skate which can't be put on when you get to the pond, or one which drags behind your foot by the strap, is worse than no skate at all.
3. If you are sure that you are ready, get on your feet and skate.

On the same subject, Scribners might bring to light something that Stevenson had written to a young friend about to take his first lesson in skating, reading as follows:

"To know the secret of skating is, indeed, I have always thought, the beginning of winter-long pleasance. It comes as sweet deliverance from the tedium of indoor isolation and brings exhilaration, now with a swift glide to the right, now with a deft swerve to the left, now with a deep breath of healthy air, now with a long exhalation of ozone, which the lungs, like greedy misers, have cast aside after draining it of its treasure. But it is not health that we love nor exhilaration that we seek, though we may think so; our design and our sufficient reward is to verify our own existence, say what you will.

"And so, my dear young friend, I would say to you: Open up your heart; sing as you skate; sing inharmoniously if you will, but sing! A man may skate with all the skill in the world; he may glide forward with incredible deftness and curve backward with divine grace, and yet if he be not master of his emotions as well as of his feet, I would say — and here Fate steps in — that he has failed."

There is, of course, plenty of good advice in the Stevenson book. But it is much better as pure reading matter than as advice to the young idea or even the middle-aged idea. It may have been all right for Stevenson to "play the sedulous ape" and consciously imitate the style of Hazlitt, Lamb, Montaigne and the rest, but if the rest of us were to try it there would result a terrible plague of insufferably artificial and affected authors, all playing the sedulous ape and all looking the part.

On the whole, the Stevenson book makes good reading and Miss Klickmann gives good advice.

LVIII

" THE EFFECTIVE SPEAKING
VOICE "

JOSEPH A. MOSHER begins his book on " The
Effective Speaking Voice " by saying:
" Among the many developments of the great war
was a widespread activity in public speaking."

Mr. Mosher, to adopt a technical term of elocu-
tion, has said a mouthful. Whatever else the war
did for us, it raised overnight an army of public
speakers among the civilian population, many of
whom seem not yet to have received their discharge.
It is the aim of Mr. Mosher's book to keep this
Landwehr in fighting trim and aid in recruiting its
ranks, possibly against the next war. Until every
nation on earth has subjected its public speakers
to a devastating operation on the larynx no true
disarmament can be said to have taken place.

In the first place there are exercises which must
be performed by the man who would have an effective speaking voice, exercises similar to Walter
Camp's Daily Dozen. You stand erect, with the

chest held moderately high. (Moderation in all things is the best rule to follow, no matter what you are doing.) Place the thumbs just above the hips, with the fingers forward over the waist to note the muscular action. Then you inhale and exhale and make the sound of " ah " and the sound of " ah-oo-oh," and, if you aren't self-conscious, you say " wah-we-wi-wa," slowly, ten or a dozen times.

" The student should stop at once if signs of dizziness appear," says the book, but it does not say whether the symptoms are to be looked for in the student himself or in the rest of the family.

The author does the public a rather bad turn when he suggests to student speakers that, under stress, they might use what is known as the " orotund." The orotund quality in public speaking is saved for passages containing grandeur of thought, when the orator feels the need of a larger, fuller, more resonant and sounding voice to be in keeping with the sentiment. Its effect is somewhat that of a chant, and here is how you do it:

The chest is raised and tensed, the cavities of the mouth and pharynx are enlarged, more breath is directed into the nasal chambers and the lips are opened more widely to give free passage to the increased volume of voice.

LOVE CONQUERS ALL

The effectiveness of the orotund might be somewhat reduced if the audience knew the conscious
mechanical processes which went to make it up. Or
if, in the Congressional Record, instead of (laughter
and applause) the vocal technique of the orator
could be indicated, how few would be the wars into
which impassioned Senators could plunge us! For
example, Mr. Thurston's plea for intervention in
Cuba:

" The time for action has come. (Tensing the
chest.) No greater reason for it can exist tomorrow
than exists today. (Enlarging the cavities of the
mouth.) Every hour's delay only adds another
chapter to the awful story of misery and death.
(Enlarging the cavities of the pharynx.) Only one
power can intervene — the United States of America. (Directing more breath into the nasal chambers.) Ours is the one great nation of the New
World — the mother of republics. (Elevating the
diaphragm.) We cannot refuse to accept this responsibility which the God of the Universe has
placed upon us as the one great power in the New
World. We must act! (Raising the tongue and
thrusting it forward so that the edges of the blade
are pressed against the upper grinders.) What
shall our action be? (Lifting the voice-box very
high and the edges of the tongue blade against the

[288]

soft palate, leaving only a small central groove for the passage of air.) "

The aspirate quality, or whisper, is very effective when well handled, and the book gives a few exercises for practice's sake. Try whispering a few of them, if you are sure that you are alone in the room. You will sound very silly if you are overheard.

a. " I can't tell just how it happened; I think the beam fell on me."

b. " Keep back; wait till I see if the coast is clear."

c. " Ask the man next to you if he'll let me see his programme."

d. " Hark! What was that? "

e. " It's too steep — he'll never make it — oh, this is terrible! "

For the cheery evening's reading, if you happen to be feeling low in your mind, let me recommend that section of " The Effective Speaking Voice " which deals with " the Subdued Range." The selections for the practice-reading include the following well-known nuggets in lighter vein:

" The Wounded Soldier," " The Death of Molly Cass," " The Little Cripple's Garden," " The Burial of Little Nell," " The Light of Other Days," " The Baby is Dead," " King David Mourns for Absalom," and " The Days That Are No More."

After all, a good laugh never does anyone any harm.

LIX

THOSE DANGEROUSLY DYNAMIC
BRITISH GIRLS

IT is difficult to get into Rose Macaulay's " Dangerous Ages " once you discover that it is going to be about another one of those offensively healthy English families.   Ever since " Mr. Britling " we have been deluged with accounts from overseas of whole droves of British brothers and sisters, mothers and fathers, grandfathers and grandmothers, who all get out at six in the morning and play hockey all over the place.   Each has some strange, intimate name like " Bim," or " Pleda," or " Goots," and you can never tell which are the brothers and which the sisters until they begin to have children along in the tenth or eleventh chapter.

In " Dangerous Ages " they swim.   Dozens of them, all in the same family, go splashing in at once and persist in calling out health slogans to one another across the waves.   There are *Neville* and *Rodney* and *Gerda* and *Kay,* and one or two very old ladies whose relationship to the rest of the clan is never very definitely established.   Grandma, for some reason or other, doesn't go in swimming that day, doubtless because she had already been in before breakfast and her suit wasn't dry.

These dynamic British girls are always full of ruddy health and current information. They go about kidding each other on the second reading of the Home Rule bill or fooling in their girlish way about the chances of the Labor candidate in the coming Duncastershire elections. It is getting so that no novel of British life will be complete without somewhere in its pages a scene like the following:

" A chance visitor at The Beetles some autumn morning along about five o'clock might have been surprised to see a trail of dog-trotting figures winding their way heatedly across the meadow. No one but a chance visitor would be surprised, however, for it was well known to invited guests that the entire Willetts family ran cross-country down to the outskirts of London and back every morning before breakfast, a matter of fourteen miles. In the lead was, of course, Dungeon in running costume, followed closely by the flaxen-haired Mid and snub-nosed Boola, then Arlix and Linny, striving valiantly for fourth place but not reckoning on the fleet-footed Meeda, who was no longer content to hobble in the vanguard with Grandpa Willetts and Grandpa's old mother, who still insisted on

"Why didn't you tell us that you were reading a paper on
birth control?"

cross-country running, although she had long since been put on the retired list at the Club.

" 'Oh, Linny,' called out Dungeon over her shoulder, ' you young minx!   Why didn't you tell us that you were reading a paper on Birth Control at the next meeting of the Spiddix? Twiller just told me today.   It's too ripping of you! "

" ' Silly goose,' panted Linny, stumbling over a hedgerow, ' how about what the vicar said the other night about your inferiority complex?   It was toppo, and you know it.'

" ' It won't be long now before we'll have disenfranchisement through, anyway,' muttered Grandpa Willetts, crashing down into a stone quarry, at which exhibition of reaction a loud chorus of laughter went up from the entire family, who by this time had reached Nogroton and were bursting with health."

LX

BOOKS AND OTHER THINGS

FOR those to whom the purple-and-gold filigreed covers of Florence L. Barclay's books bring a stirring of the sap and a fluttering of the susceptible heart, " Returned Empty " comes as a languorous relief from the stolid realism of most present-day writing. One reads it and swoons. And on opening one's eyes again, one hears old family retainers murmuring in soft retentive accents: " Here, sip some of this, my lord; 'twill bring the roses back to those cheeks and the strength to those poor limbs." It's elegant, that's all there is to it, elegant.

"Returned Empty " was the inscription on the wrappings which enfolded the tiny but aristocratic form of a man-child left on the steps of the Foundlings Institution one moonless October night. There was also some reference to Luke, xii., 6, which in return refers to five sparrows sold for two farthings. What more natural, then, than for the matron to name the little one Luke Sparrow?

BOOKS AND OTHER THINGS

Luke was an odd boy but refined. So odd that he used to go about looking in at people's windows when they forgot to pull down the shades, and so refined that he never wished to be inside with them.

But one night, when he was thirty years old, he looked in at the window of a very refined and elegant mansion and saw a woman. In the simple words of the author, " in court or cottage alike she would be queen." That's the kind of woman she was.

And what do you think? She saw Luke looking in. Not only saw him but came over to the window and told him that she had been expecting him. Well, you could have knocked Luke over with a feather. However, he allowed himself to be ushered in by the butler (everything in the house was elegant like that) and up to a room where he found evening clothes, bath-salts and grand things of that nature. On passing a box of books which stood in the hall he read the name on it " before he realized what he was doing." Of course the minute he thought what an unrefined thing it was to do he stopped, but it was too late. He had already seen that his hostess's name was " Lady Tintagel."

When later he met her down in the luxurious dining-room she was just as refined as ever. And so was he. They both were so refined that she had to tell the butler to "serve the fruit in the Oak Room, Thomas."

Once in the Oak Room she told him her strange tale. It seemed that he was her husband. He didn't remember it, but he was. He had been drowned some years before and she had wished so hard that he might come back to life that finally he had been born again in the body of Luke Sparrow. It's funny how things work out like that sometimes.

But Luke, who, as has been said before, was an odd boy, took it very hard and said that he didn't want to be brought back to life. Not even when she told him that his name was now Sir Nigel Guido Cadross Tintagel, Bart. He became very cross and said that he was going out and drown himself all over again, just to show her that she shouldn't have gone meddling with his spirit life. He was too re-fined to say so, but when you consider that he was just thirty, and his wife, owing to the difference in time between the spirit world and this, had gone on growing old until she was now pushing sixty, he had a certain amount of justice on his side. But of course she was Lady Tintagel, and all the lovers of Florence Barclay will understand that that is some-thing.

So, after reciting Tennyson's " Crossing the Bar,"

at her request (credit is given in the front of the book for the use of this poem, and only rightly too, for without it the story could never have been written), he goes out into the ocean. But there — we mustn't give too much of the plot away. All that one need know is that Luke or Sir Nigel, as you wish (and what reader of Florence Barclay wouldn't prefer Sir Nigel?), was so cultured that he said, " Nobody in the whole world knows it, save you and I," and referred to " flotsam and jetson " as he was swimming out into the path of the rising sun. " Jetsam " is such an ugly word.

It is only fitting that on his tombstone Lady Tintagel should have had inscribed an impressive and high-sounding misquotation from the Bible.

LXI

"MEASURE YOUR MIND"

MEASURE Your Mind" by M. R. Traube and Frank Parker Stockbridge, is apt to be a very discouraging book if you have any doubt at all about your own mental capacity. From a hasty glance through the various tests I figure it out that I would be classified in Group B, indicating "Low Average Ability," reserved usually for those just learning to speak the English language and preparing for a career of holding a spike while another man hits it. If they ever adopt the "menti-meter tests" on this journal I shall last just about forty-five minutes.

And the trouble is that each test starts off so easily. You begin to think that you are so good that no one has ever appreciated you. There is for instance, a series of twenty-four pictures (very badly drawn too, Mr. Frank Parker Stockbridge. You think you are so smart, picking flaws with people's intelligence. If I couldn't draw a better head than the one on page 131 I would throw up the whole business). At any rate, in each one of these pictures there is something wrong (wholly apart from the drawing). You are supposed to pick out the incongruous feature, and you have 180 seconds in which to tear the twenty-four pictures to pieces.

The first one is easy. The rabbit has one human ear. In the second one the woman's eye is in her hair. Pretty soft, you say to yourself. In the third the bird has three legs. It looks like a cinch. Following in quick succession come a man with his mouth in his forehead, a horse with cow's horns, a mouse with rabbit's ears, etc. You will have time for a handspring before your 180 seconds are up.

But then they get tricky. There is a post-card with a stamp upside down. Well, what's wrong with that? Certainly there is no affront to nature in a stamp upside down. Neither is there in a man's looking through the large end of a telescope if he wants to. You can't arbitrarily say at the top of the page, "Mark the thing that is wrong," and then have a picture of a house with one window larger than all the others and expect any one to agree with you that it is necessarily *wrong*. It may look queer, but so does the whole picture. You can't tell; the big window may open from a room that needs a big window. I am not going to stultify

myself by making things wrong about which I
know none of the facts. Who am I that I should
condemn a man for looking through the large end
of a telescope? Personally, I like to look through
the large end of a telescope. It only shows the
state of personal liberty in this country when a picture of a man looking at a ship through the large
end of a telescope is held before the young and
branded as " wrong."

Arguing these points with yourself takes up quite
a bit of time and you get so out of patience with the
man that made up the examination that you lose
all heart in it.

Then come some pictures about which I am
frankly in the dark. There is a Ford car with a
rather funny-looking mud-guard, but who can pick
out any one feature of a Ford and say that it is
wrong? It may look wrong but I'll bet that the
car in this picture as it stands could pass many a
big car on a hill.

Then there is a boy holding a bat, and while his
position isn't all that a coach could ask, the only
radically wrong thing that I can detect about the
picture is that he is evidently playing baseball in a
clean white shirt with a necktie and a rather natty
cap set perfectly straight on his head. It is true

he has his right thumb laid along the edge of the bat, but maybe he likes to bunt that way. There is something in the picture that I don't get, I am afraid, just as there is in the picture of two men playing golf. One is about to putt. Aside from the fact that his putter seems just a trifle long, I should have to give up my guess and take my defeat like a man.

But I do refuse to concede anything on Picture No. 22. Here a baby is shown sitting on the floor. He appears to be about a year and a half old. Incidentally, he is a very plain baby. Strewn about him on the floor are the toys that he has been playing with. There are a ball, a rattle, a ring, a doll, a bell and a pair of roller-skates. Evidently, the candidate is supposed to be aghast at the roller-skates in the possession of such a small child.

The man who drew that picture had evidently never furnished playthings for a small child. I can imagine nothing that would delight a child of a year and a half more than a pair of roller-skates to chew and spin and hit himself in the face with. They could also be dropped on Daddy when Daddy was lying on the floor in an attempt to be sociable. Of all the toys arranged before the child, the roller-skates are the most logical. I suppose that the author of this test would insist on calling a picture wrong which showed a baby with a safety-razor in his hand or an overshoe on his head, and yet a photograph of the Public Library could not be more true to life.

That is my great trouble in taking tests and examinations of any kind. I always want to argue with the examiner, because the examiner is always so obviously wrong.

LXII

THE BROW–ELEVATION IN
HUMOR

AFTER an author has been dead for some time,
it becomes increasingly difficult for his publishers to get out a new book by him each year.
Without recourse to the ouija board, Harper &
Brothers manage to do very well by Mark Twain,
considering that all they have to work with are the
books that he wrote when he was alive. Each year
we get something from the pen of the famous humorist, even though the ink has faded slightly. An
introduction by Albert Bigelow Paine and a hitherto
unpublished photograph as a frontspiece, and there
you are — the season's new Mark Twain book.

This season it is " Moments With Mark Twain,"
a collection of excerpts from his works for quick
and handy reading. We may look for further books
in this series in 1923, 1924, 1925, &c., to be entitled
" Half Hours With Mark Twain " (the selections
a trifle longer), " Pleasant Week-Ends With Mark
Twain," " Indian Summer With Mark Twain," &c.

LOVE CONQUERS ALL

There is an interesting comparison between this sample bottle of the humor of Mark Twain and that contained in the volume entitled " Something Else Again," by Franklin P. Adams. The latter is a volume of verse and burlesques which have appeared in the newspapers and magazines.

In the days when Mark Twain was writing, it was considered good form to spoof not only the classics but surplus learning of any kind. A man was popularly known as an affected cuss when he could handle anything more erudite than a nasal past participle or two in his own language, and any one who wanted to qualify as a humorist had to be able to mispronounce any word of over three syllables.

Thus we find Mark Twain, in the selections given in this volume, having amusing trouble with the pronunciation of Michael Angelo and Leonardo da Vinci, expressing surprise that Michael Angelo was dead, picking flaws in the old master's execution and complaining of the use of foreign words which have their equivalent " in a nobler language — English."

There certainly is no harm in this school of humor, and it has its earnest and prosperous exponents to-day. In fact, a large majority of the people still like to have some one poke fun at the things in which they themselves are not proficient, whether it be pronunciation, Latin or bricklaying.

But there is an increasingly large section of the reading public who, while they may not be expert in Latin composition, nevertheless do not think that a Latin word in itself is a cause for laughter. A French phrase thrown in now and then for metrical effect does not strike them as essentially an affectation, and they are willing to have references made to characters whose native language may not have been that noblest of all languages, our native tongue.

That such a school of readers exists is proved by the popularity of F. P. A's verses and prose. If any one had told Mark Twain that a man could run a daily newspaper column in New York and amass any degree of fame through translations of the "Odes of Horace " into the vernacular, the veteran humorist would probably have slapped Albert Bigelow Paine on the back and taken the next boat for Bermuda. And yet in " Something Else Again " we find some sixteen translations of Horace and other "furriners," exotic phrases such as " eheu fugaces " and " ex parte " used without making faces over them, and a popular exposition of highly technical verse forms which James Russell Lowell and Hal Longfellow would have considered terrifically high-brow.

And yet thousands of American business men quote
F. P. A. to thousands of other American business
men every morning.

Can it be said that the American people are not so
low-brow as they like to pretend? There is a great
deal of affectation in this homespun frame of mind,
and many a man makes believe that he doesn't know
things simply because no one has ever written about
them in the American Magazine. If the truth were
known, we are all a great deal better educated than
we will admit, and the derisive laughter with which
we greet signs of culture is sometimes very hollow.
In F. P. A. we find a combination which makes it
possible for us to admit our learning and still be
held honorable men. It is a good sign that his following is increasing.

LXIII

BUSINESS LETTERS

A TEXT–BOOK on English composition, giving examples of good and bad letter-writing, is always a mine of possibilities for one given to ruminating and with nothing in particular to do. In " Business Man's English " the specimen letters are unusually interesting. It seems almost as if the authors, Wallace Edgar Bartholomew and Floyd Hurlbut, had selected their examples with a view to their fiction possibilities. It also seems to the reader as if he were opening someone else's mail.

For instance, the following is given as a type of " very short letter, well placed ":

Mr. Richard T. Green,
Employment Department,
Travellers' Insurance Co.,
Chicago, Ill.

Dear Mr. Green:
The young man about whom you inquire has much native ability and while in our employ proved himself a master of office routine.

LOVE CONQUERS ALL

I regret to say, however, that he left us under circumstances that would not justify our recommending him to you.

Cordially yours,   C. S. THOMPSON

Now I want to know what those " circumstances " were. And in lieu of the facts, I am afraid that I shall have to imagine some circumstances for myself. Personally, I don't believe that the " young man " was to blame. Bad companions, maybe, or I shouldn't be at all surprised if he was shielding someone else, perhaps a young lady stenographer with whom he was in love. The more I think of it the more I am sure that this was the secret of the whole thing. You see, he was a good worker and had, Mr. Thompson admits, proved himself a master of office routine. Although Mr. Thompson doesn't say so, I have no doubt but that he would have been promoted very shortly.

And then he fell in love with a little brown-eyed stenographer. You know how it is yourself. She had an invalid mother at home and was probably trying to save enough money to send her father to college. And whatever she did, it couldn't have been so very bad, for she was such a nice girl.

Well, at any rate, it looks to me as if the young man, while he was arranging the pads of paper for the regular Monday morning conference, overheard the office-manager telling about this affair (I have good reason to believe that it was a matter of carelessness in the payroll) and saying that he considered the little brown-eyed girl dishonest.

At this the young man drew himself up to his full height and, looking the office-manager squarely in the eye, said:

"No, Mr. Hostetter; it was I who did it, and I will take the consequences. And I want it understood that no finger of suspicion shall be pointed at Agnes Fairchild, than whom no truer, sweeter girl ever lived!"

"I am sorry to hear this, Ralph," said Mr. Hostetter. "You know what this means."

"I do, sir," said Ralph, and turned to look out over the chimney-pots of the city, biting his under lip very tight.

And on Saturday Ralph left.

Since then he has applied at countless places for work, but always they have written to his old employer, Mr. Thompson, for a reference, and have received a letter similar to the one given here as an example. Naturally, they have not felt like taking him on. You cannot blame them. And, in a way, you cannot blame Mr. Thompson. You see, Mr.

LOVE CONQUERS ALL

Hostetter didn't tell Mr. Thompson all the circumstances of the affair. He just said that Ralph had confessed to responsibility for the payroll mix-up. If Mr. Thompson had been there at the time I am sure that he would have divined that Ralph was shielding Miss Fairchild, for Mr. Thompson liked Ralph. You can see that from his letter.

But as it stands now things are pretty black for the boy, and it certainly seems as if in this great city there ought to be some one who will give him a job without writing to Mr. Thompson about him. This department will be open as a clearing-house for offers of work for a young man of great native ability and master of office routine who is just at present, unfortunately, unable to give any references, but who will, I am quite sure, justify any trust that may be placed in him in the future.